pathfinder guide

Skye *and the* North West Highlands

Walk Sutherland
Tom Strang.
ISBN 09522634 0 0
Highlands of Scotland
Tom's Book

W A L K S

Compiled by
John Brooks
and Neil Wilson

KT-479-921

JARROLD

Ordnance Survey

Acknowledgements
The author would like to thank Malcolm Morrison of the
Forestry Commission on Skye and Ronnie Nicholson of
Raasay for their help in the compilation of this guide.

Text:	John Brooks, Neil Wilson
Photography:	John Brooks, Neil Wilson
Editor:	Donald Greig
Designers:	Brian Skinner, Doug Whitworth
Mapping:	Heather Pearson, Tina Shaw

Series Consultant: Brian Conduit

Jarrold Publishing   ISBN 0-7117-0850-9

First published 1996 by Jarrold Publishing and Ordnance
Survey. Reprinted 1998
Printed in Great Britain by Jarrold Printing, Thetford 2/98

Jarrold Publishing
Whitefriars, Norwich NR3 1TR
Ordnance Survey
Romsey Road, Southampton SO16 4GU

Front cover:	The Quiraing, Skye
Previous page:	The Old Man of Stoer

Contents

The Law and Tradition as they affect Walking in Scotland; Scotland's Hills and Mountains: a Concordat on Access; Safety on the Hills; Glossary of Gaelic Names; Useful Organisations; Ordnance Survey Maps

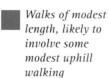

Short, easy walks

Walks of modest length, likely to involve some modest uphill walking

More challenging walks which may be longer and/or over more rugged terrain, often with some stiff climbs

Keymap 1

SCALE 1:312 500 or 1 INCH to 5 MILES *1CM to 3.1 KM*
KEYMAP HEIGHTS SHOWN IN FEET

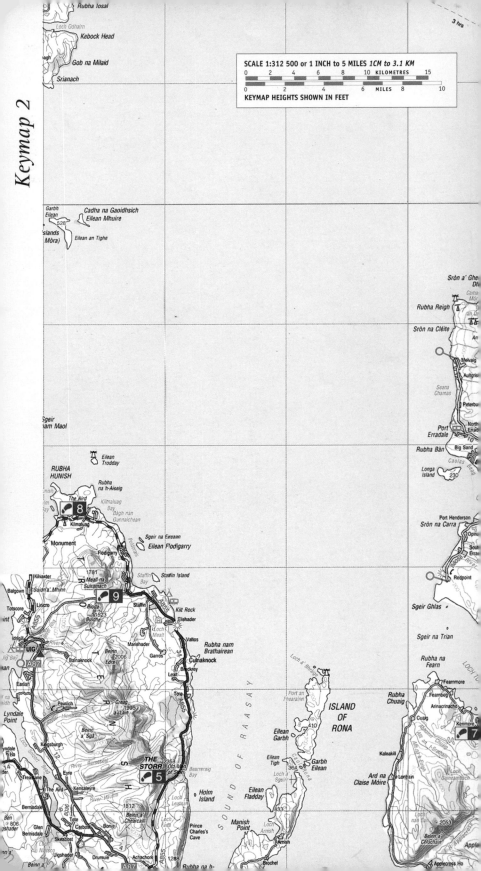

Camas
Eilean Ghlais
Rubha Mór
Rubh' a' Choin
Reiff
Brae of Achnahaird
Altandhu
Achiltibuie
262
641
Inverpolly Lodge
Inver...
Inver Na...

Eilean Mullagrach
Isle Ristol
234
669
Polbain
Loch Osgaig
Aird of Coigach
Inverpolly Forest
Stac Pollaidh 2009

Glas-leac Mór
Badentarbat Bay
Achnahaird
Polglass
1605
1973

Tanera Beg 268
Summer Isles
406
Tanera Mór
Achduart
BEN MÓR COIGACH 2438
C O I G A C...

Glas-leac Beag
Horse Island
Culnacraig
Geodha Mór
2438
Strath...

Priest Island
Eilean Dubh
Càrn nan Sgeir
Camas Mór

Greenstone Point
Cailleach Head
Leac Dhonn
Isle Martin 397
947 Crea...
h-lo...

Rubha Beag
4
Stattic Point
480 Scoraig
Annat Bay
Rhue
Ardmair
UI...

Opinan
Rubha Mór
Mellon Udrigle
Carnach
Rireavach
Beinn Ghobhlach 2082
Badrallach

Gob a' Chuaille
478
Achgarve
GRUINARD BAY
Gruinard Island 345
607
Badluarach
Mungasdale
Beinn a' Chaisgein...
Badcaul

Eilean Furadh Mór
Beinn 513 Dearg Mhór
Mellon Charles
Laide
Gruinard House
Inchina
Dundonnell
39
Camusnagaul
Hotel

24
Cove
Ormiscaig
Bualnaluib
Sand
Coast
Little Gruinard
17
985
Ardessie
Sail Mhór 2508
2293
Dundonnell
Dundonnell House
1193

Tighnafiline
Aultbea
Drumchork
Beinn Dearg Bad Chailleach
897
Loch Fada
1283
Carn nam Buailtean
2493
Strathnasheallag Forest
3484
AN TEALLACH
28

Isle of Ewe 233
Loch Bhad Achnaich
1139
Fisherfield Forest
2974
Beinn Dearg Mór
Strath na Sealga
Dundonnell Forest
1820

LOCH EWE
Inverasdale
593
Aird Dhubh
Beinn a' Chaisgein Beag 2230
Beinn a' Chlàisgein Mór 2802
Beinn a' Chlaidheimh 3194
2647

Midtown
Rubha' Ard na Bà
Tournaig
Meall na Mèine 820
Bad Bog
2595
Beinn Airigh Charr
3326
Mullach Coire Mhic Fhearchair

Naast
Brae
Poolewe
Lòndubh
749
Loch Kernsary
2817
Beinn Làir
Letterewe Forest
Loch Garbhaig
2424
Groban
327...
A' Chai...

Strath
Gairloch
1140
5
Loch Tollaidh
1123
1381 Meall an Doirein
Eilean Subhainn
Letterewe
3215
SLIOCH
1365
2333 Beinn nan Ramh

12
Charlestown
Kerrysdale
Loch Bad an Sgalaig
1319
Talladale
B8056
A832
LOCH MAREE
Rhu Iuba 2231
Beinn a' Mhuinidh
Kinlochewe Forest
Heights of Kinlochewe
Lochrosque

11
Shieldaig
River Kerry
961
Flowerdale Forest
2805
Beinn an Eòin
2882 Meall Ghiubhais
Anancaun
Incheril
3062 Fionn Bheinn

Eilean Horrisdale
2869
Shieldaig Forest
2031 Beinn Bhreac
Ruadh-stac 2313
2378
Kinlochewe
Carn a' Ghlinne 1768
Carn Beag 1804
Achnasheen

Lower Diabaig
3232 Beinn Alligin
BEINN EIGHE
3456
Coulin Lodge
Badavanich
Loch a' Chroisg
An Liathanach
Loch Gowan

25
Rechullin
22
Torridon Forest
Torridon Ho
LIATHACH
Glen Torridon
Spidean 2566 Coire nan Clach
Coulin
2223 Carn Breac
Ledgowan Forest
3026
Carn Mh...

Alligin Shuas
Inveralligin
16
Sgurr Dubh 2566
Coulin Forest
Glen Carron
Glencarron Lodge
Carn Gorm

UPPER LOCH TORRIDON
Annat
2313
Glencarron and Glenuig Forest

2
Shieldaig
Balgy
Ben-damph Forest
Beinn Damh 2957
3060
Beinn Liath Mhór
Sgorr Ruadh 3142
Craig
Achnashellach Station
2830
Spurr a'...
3304

Glenshieldaig Forest
1692
Maol Chean-dearg
2410
Achnashellach Forest
Balnacra
Coulags
Maoile Lunndaidh 3304

Loch Coultrie
1682

Keymap 3

SCALE 1:312 500 or 1 INCH to 5 MILES *1CM to 3.1 KM*

0 2 4 6 8 10 KILOMETRES 15

0 2 4 6 MILES 8 10

KEYMAP HEIGHTS SHOWN IN FEET

Handa

Bi
Meall

Point of Stoer
Cirean Geardail
Rubha nan Còsan
Sgeir nan Gall
Oldany Island
336
530
Culkein
Eilean Chrona
Clashnessie Bay
6
Annacarnin
Cluas Deas
Clashmore
Clashnessie · 337
Balchladich
Rienachait
Rubh' a' Mhill Dheirg
Bay of Stoer
Stoer
ClachToll
681
Rubha Leumair
Achmelvich Bay
Rhicarn
Achmelvich
Rubha Rodha
Baddidarach
360
Loch
Soyea Island
Loch Inver
Kirkaig Point
Loch Oula
A' Chleit
Strathan
Inverkirkaig
Loch Kirkaig
Rubha na Brèige
814
Rubha Coigeach
Eilean Mór
ENARD BAY
Camas Coille
Camas Eilean Ghlais
262
Rubha Mór
Rubh' a' Choin
Reiff
Brae of Achnahaird
Inverpolly Lodge
Altandhu
Loch Osgaig
Aird of Coigach
Inv
F
St
Eilean Mullagrach
234
Isle Ristol
669
Polbain
Loch Bad a' Ghaill
Glas-leac Mór
Achiltibuie
Badentarbat Bay
Polglass
Tanera Beg 268
406
1605
19
S u m m e r I s l e s
Tanera Mór
BEN MÓR COIGACH
2438
Glas-leac Beag
Horse Island
Horse Sound
Achduart
Geodha Mór
Eilean Dubh
Priest Island
Bottle Island
Càrn nan Sgeir
Camas Mór
Leac Dhonn
Isle Martin
397
L
Kana
Greenstone Point
Cailleach Head
Annat Bay
Rhue
Rubha Beag
Stattic Point
480
Scoraig
Camach
Opiran
4
Gob a' Chuaille
Rubha Mór
Mellon Udrigle
Gruinard
Island 345
607
L I T T L E L
Rieavach
Benn Ghobhlach
Slaggan
478

Keymap 3

At-a-glance...

Walk	Page	Start	Distance	Time	Highest Point
Ardheslaig on the Applecross Peninsula	28	Kenmore	4½ miles (7.25km)	2½ hrs	492ft (150m)
Armadale Castle Estate	20	Armadale Castle, south Skye	2¾ miles (4.5km)	2 hrs	614ft (187m)
Beinn na Caillich Horseshoe	60	north-west of Broadford, Skye	5 miles) (8km	5 hrs	2400ft (732m)
Camasunary, Elgol and Glasnakille	80	south-west of Kirkibost Skye	9½ miles (15.25km)	6 hrs	623ft (190m)
Circuit of Beinn Alligin	67	2 miles (3.25km) west of Torridon	8 miles (12.75km)	5½ hrs	2000ft (610m)
Coire Làgan and Eas Mór	46	Glen Brittle, west Skye	5½ miles (8.75km)	4½ hrs	1800ft (550m)
Coire Mhic Fhearchair	48	Glen Torridon	8 miles (12.9km)	5 hrs	1935ft (509m)
Eas a' Chùal Aluinn	54	south of Kylesku off A894	7 miles (11.25km)	4½ hrs	886ft (270m)
Fairy Lochs from Shieldaig	36	near Shieldaig on B8056	5 miles (8km)	2½ hrs	328ft (100m)
Fairy Pools and Coire na Creiche	41	Glen Brittle Forest, west Skye	5½ miles (8.75km)	3½ hrs	1128ft (344m)
Flowerdale Waterfalls, Gairloch	38	Charlestown village	5 miles (8km)	3½ hrs	820ft (250m)
Glen Brittle and Glen Eynort	56	Eynort village, west Skye	10½ miles (16.75km)	4½ hrs	1063ft (324m)
Inverianvie and Gruinard Rivers	51	on A832 east of Laide	6½ miles (10.5km)	3½ hrs	656ft (200m)
Loch an Draing and Camas Mór from Cove	74	Cove, Loch Ewe, off B8057	10 miles (16km)	6 hrs	120ft (55m)
Loch na Sealga and Gleann Chaorachain	87	south of Dundonnell, off the A832	11 miles (17.5km)	6 hrs	1312ft (400m)
Lower Diabaig and Leacan Bàna from Inveralligin	77	Inveralligin, Loch Torridon	8½ miles (13.5km)	5½ hrs	836ft (255m)
Mellon Udrigle	22	Mellon Udrigle, Gruinard Bay	3 miles (4.75km)	1¼ hrs	187ft (57m)
Point of Sleat	34	Aird of Sleat, south Skye	5 miles (8km)	4 hrs	295ft (90m)
Point of Stoer	26	Stoer lighthouse	4½ miles (7.25km)	1½ hrs	528ft (161m)
The Quiraing	32	Uig–Staffin road, north Skye	4½ miles (7.25km)	3 hrs	1739ft (530m)
Raasay – Dùn Caan and the Burma Road	84	ferry pier, Raasay	10 miles (16km)	6 hrs	1470ft (448m)
Ramasaig, Lorgill and the Hoe	44	Ramasaig, north-west Skye	5 miles (8km)	3 hrs	722ft (220m)
Rubh' an Dùnain from Glen Brittle	71	Glen Brittle campsite, west Skye	8½ miles (13.5km)	5 hrs	394ft (120m)
Rubha Hunish	30	Duntulm, north Skye	4½ miles (7.25km)	3 hrs	1092ft (333m)
The Sanctuary and the Old Man of Storr	24	north of Portree, Skye, on A855	3 miles (4.75km)	2½ hrs	1476ft (450m)
Sandwood Bay	63	Blairmore, near Kinlochbervie	9 miles (14.5km)	4½ hrs	436ft (133m)
Shieldaig	18	Shieldaig, Torridon	2½ miles (4km)	1½ hrs	148ft (45m)
Torvaig and The Bile from Portree	16	Portree, Skye	2½ miles (4km)	1½ hrs	394ft (120m)

Comments

A figure-of-eight route which uses parts of a mountain road as well as an ancient hillside path and gives glorious views of the coastline and mountains surrounding Loch Torridon.

The walk passes through the gardens and parkland of one of Skye's most famous demesnes. The climax of the route is at a hilltop viewpoint giving outstanding views of the island and mainland.

The wonderful curving ridge which is the main attraction of this route is only reached after a steep and wearying climb through a boulder field. There is also an exciting scree descent.

This walk approaches the threshold of the Cuillins, but then leaves the mountains to follow lochside shores. There are clear paths or country roads for most of the way.

A compass and good visibility are essential for this memorable walk which climbs through Bealach a'Chomhla on the flanks of Beinn Alligin – truly wild and beautiful countryside.

The outward part follows a famous access route into the heart of the Cuillins – a hard slog of over 1800ft (550m) to a wildly beautiful corrie loch overlooked by scree slopes and rocky crags.

A rewarding walk deep into the Torridon Hills to visit some of Scotland's most spectacular mountain scenery. Most of the walk is on a well-made path, but the last $\frac{1}{2}$ mile (800m) to the corrie is rougher.

Considerable effort is needed to climb to the top of Britain's highest free-falling waterfall. You really need a clear day after heavy rain to view the scenery at its best.

The start of this walk is at the northern Shieldaig, on the B8056, not to be confused with the village on Loch Torridon. It is an excellent moorland walk visiting the site of a wartime aircrash.

The Fairy Pools in Glen Brittle are where the Little People of Skye are supposed to bathe, in a stream which can be awesome when the snows melt or after heavy rain.

The outward walk to the waterfalls is straightforward but the suggested return route, over pathless hillside, is more demanding. The beautiful beach at the start may prove irresistible to children.

This is a level forest walk giving views of the Cuillins and Loch Eynort and makes an excellent excursion if you are feeling jaded, or if the weather is wet and/or windy (which even happens on Skye!)

A compass is required for this walk as there is rough country between the two rivers without distinctive landmarks. Once this part of the walk is over the way back is on the banks of a famous salmon river.

You are never far from the sea on this walk, but there are still times when you could find navigation difficult. Camas Mór lies at the end of the walk, a wide beach reached by an easy path down the cliff.

Few walks encapsulate the desolate beauty of the north-west better than this route which follows a faint path below the buttresses of An Teallach to reach remote Loch na Sealga.

Places where sea meets mountain are not rare in western Scotland but this walk gives you the chance of seeing this in perfection. The walking is over steep, rough ground for much of the way.

The start is from a crofting township with a fine beach which overlooks Gruinard Bay. The walk passes an estuary to reach rugged cliffs famous for colonies of seabirds – remember to take binoculars.

Do not hurry this delightful walk on Sleat, the southernmost part of Skye. It provides two destinations, and either of them would make ideal places to picnic and enjoy far-reaching coastal views.

The Assynt peninsula has a wonderful coastline which culminates in the Point of Stoer. The clifftop path passes above The Old Man of Stoer, a famous rock stack which is a favourite venue for climbers.

The amazing rockshapes of the Quiraing were formed by a landslip at the end of the Ice Age. This walk passes through them and climbs to give magnificent views of the north of Skye.

Get over to Raasay as early as you can for this walk passes through some difficult (albeit very beautiful) countryside. The summit of Dùn Caan is one of the finest viewpoints in western Scotland.

A clear track leads to beautiful Lorgill where once a crofting community flourished. The return provides more energetic walking on the heather-covered clifftop which gives grand seascapes. No dogs.

The destination of this walk is a romantic clifftop fort which could be called the Scottish Tintagel. For much of the way you will be on pathless moorland though it is hard to get lost with the sea so close.

Although the path down to Hunish from the clifftop looks fearsome, the descent is easy after the initial rock staircase. The route without this optional extra remains very enjoyable.

Although only a short distance is covered, the gradient is steep and much of the ground very wet. The reward makes it worthwhile, The Sanctuary being a place of great peace and spectacular landforms.

The fame of this wonderful beach is spreading and days when you can enjoy it all to yourself are rare. The way to the beach is via the clifftop where you will encounter few other walkers.

A delightful seaside walk which allows you to appreciate the majesty of the mountains on the far side of Loch Torridon. The path is over rough ground for some of the way.

This short walk provides a gentle introduction to walking on Skye. The shoreline path rounds a headland to give views of the high cliffs to the north before returning through farmland.

At-a-glance...

Introduction to Skye and the North West Highlands

This Pathfinder Guide covers a substantial area of Scotland's western seaboard. The southernmost walks are based on Gairloch and Torridon, while Sandwood Bay, the location of the most northern route, lies 75 miles (120km) to the north-east. The walks divide simply into mountain and coastal routes, though there are few that fail to provide views of the sea at some point. Sea views are the icing on the cake in many of the hill walks too, some of which take you deep into a lonely countryside of lochs and mountains. All the routes follow tracks and paths for much of the way but there are occasions when some of them strike across heather where there are only sheep-tracks. In these instances the direction to walk is usually obvious, but anyone using this book should be aware that Highland weather can easily change drastically in an hour or so. For this reason suitable footwear and clothing is essential, and you should also be equipped with a compass, torch, whistle and first-aid kit as well as energy-giving spare rations.

The haunted croft at Sandwood Bay

In most places in Skye and the North-West Highlands there is an abundance of high-quality water in springs and burns where you can refill water bottles. However, there may be occasions on the coast or high on bare mountains where it is difficult to replenish supplies. Yet the main danger is rather in there being too much water for the walker to ford certain burns and rivers. For this reason – as well as for comfort and safety – be sure that you have a current weather forecast before setting out. Mountaincall for Western Scotland is on 0891 500441.

The North West Mainland

A bridge now spans the neck of Loch a' Chairn Bhàin at Kylesku, replacing a famous ferry service. This point marks an important geological division in the North-West Highlands, a classic area for studying the structure of landforms. To the north, the rock is gneiss, which appears exceptionally bare as it does not support heather even though coarse grass and sedge will grow. Gneiss is an abrasive rock, particularly hard on walking-boots. The landscape of north-west Sutherland abounds in lochans where water-lilies and water lobelias thrive, but away from the coastline with its succession of sea lochs the main impression is of bare desolation. In the extreme north, the coast becomes spectacular, with huge cliffs facing the Atlantic breakers between Sandwood Bay and Cape Wrath.

The main road follows the shore of Loch Broom south via Ullapool to Strath More and the Corrieshalloch Gorge, where the Falls of Measach are a famous tourist attraction. At this point a road leaves westwards to Dundonnell and Little Loch Broom. This provides access to many of the mainland walks in this book as it follows the irregular coastline westwards before swinging to the south to Gairloch and Loch Maree.

At the southern end of Loch Maree the road divides, the right-hand fork striking westwards into Glen Torridon. The trio of fine mountains on the north side of the glen provides some of the best walking in Scotland. Beinn Eighe, Liathach and Beinn Alligin are three Munros that can tax the strength and skills of the most experienced rock-climber or hillwalker. They are seen at their best as you drive along the coastal road from Applecross – great mountains that appear to rise almost sheer from the waters of the loch. In high summer their tops still look as though they carry a light covering of snow but this is deceptive as it is actually the Cambrian quartzite that glitters above the glowing red sandstone of the lower slopes. The latter is a comparatively young rock, having been laid down only 800 million years ago, at the time when Europe was still joined to America. The gneiss mentioned earlier, which also outcrops in Torridon, is amongst the oldest of all rocks, having erupted from the earth's core at some time around 1700 million years before this.

Isle of Skye

It remains to be seen whether Skye will lose any of its magic and romance now that a bridge links the island to the mainland, but this hardly affects its matchless scenery. Many writers have commented on the aptness of the name for a place where the sky is ever-changing and forms a vital part of the landscape of mountain, moor and water. There are certainly differences of opinion concerning the derivation of the name. Some claim it comes from the Norse and means 'the clouded isle', and this would certainly be appropriate in view of the climate, but others think it comes from another Norse word meaning a 'shield'. A further theory puts forward the Gaelic word sgiath, meaning 'a wing', and this may be supported by its appearance on a map, though how its early inhabitants could know of its shape is not explained.

Rowan berries are an emblem of the Highlands.

There can be no such disagreements about the quality of Skye's scenery. The Cuillins are the heights that lie almost at the centre of the island and form what has been described as 'the most exciting skyline in Britain'. Their dramatic outline can be seen from many points. The Black Cuillins have the most spectacular peaks and ridges and are made of gabbro, a tough volcanic rock loved by climbers and scramblers. Glaciers gouged out the great corries, which give the ridges and sheer faces favoured by climbers.

Liathach from Loch Clair

In contrast, the Red Hills, which neighbour the Cuillins, are made of pink granite that breaks down into scree, which, while fun to descend, is almost impossible to climb. Blà Bheinn (or Blaven) is dominant amongst the western Red Hills, as is Beinn na Caillich to the east, with its magnificent ridge walk.

Other landmarks on Skye are almost as distinctive in appearance as the Cuillin Mountains. The Old Man of Storr is to be seen on the drive northwards from Sligachan to Portree, an amazing pinnacle that seems to defy gravity and looks as if it is on the verge of toppling. A little further to the north is the Quiraing, which, like Storr, was formed by a catastrophic landslip during the end of the Ice Age and has similar features. Although the Old Man of Storr is now stable, geologists maintain that the Quiraing continues to slip seawards.

Rubha Hunish is an unobtrusive landmark forming the northern tip of Skye, a tiny peninsula that can be reached only by descending 300-foot- (90 m) high cliffs. It is an intensely beautiful spot, which will appeal to anyone with a sense of poetry or a love of wild places. There are many other similar spots on the island, which lie away from the tourist routes and can be reached only by walkers.

Apart from Prince Charles Edward Stuart, Dr Johnson was the most celebrated eighteenth-century visitor to Skye. His main interest was in the people inhabiting the island and the way they lived, and he failed to appreciate the scenic qualities of the island, remarking:
'No part that I have seen is plain, you are always climbing or descending, and every step is upon rock or mire. A walk upon ploughed ground in England is a dance upon carpets, compared to the toilsome drudgery of wandering in Skye. ...'

Deer Stalking

Deer stalking still provides much-needed income for the region and is a necessary sport. Since the slaying of the last wolf in the seventeenth century, deer have had no natural predator. Thus numbers have to be controlled or the animals either starve or may damage agricultural land as they seek food from a wider area. The time for shooting stags is critical, usually lasting from mid-August to mid-October, when their antlers have stopped growing and the animals are at their best. Once the autumn rut has started they quickly lose condition. On most estates in the area walkers have unrestricted access unless stalking is in progress. In the season there are usually notices at points of access to warn when shooting is to take place, but the onus is also on the walker to make sure the route is clear before starting out. Where possible, telephone numbers are listed with the routes that may be affected by stalking. Tourist information offices will also tell you about stalking restrictions.

Lambing Time

Walkers with dogs will not be welcomed on land crossed by many of these walks between mid-April and the end of May. This particularly applies to coastal routes, where pastureland often extends down to the fine turf fringing the clifftops and beaches. Shepherds view any dog running free with justifiable suspicion at any time of the year, and if a dog is seen to be chasing sheep it can be shot. It is therefore important to keep your animal under close control and on a lead if you are walking near sheep. The introduction to each walk warns of any potential problems and of walks where notices ban dogs from the land (though these are becoming more numerous, and some may have been erected after this book was published).

Achnacloich in the south of Skye

Torvaig and The Bile from Portree

Start	At the road end just past the drive to the Cuillin Hills Hotel, Portree, Skye
Distance	2½ miles (4km)
Approximate time	1½ hours
Parking	Parking place at the end of the shoreline road. From the A855 follow the sign to Budhmor, then the one to Cuillin Hills Hotel
Refreshments	Pubs, cafés, etc. in Portree
Ordnance Survey maps	Landranger 23 (North Skye) and Pathfinder 171, NG 44/54 (Portree)

This short walk takes you round the coast from Portree on a good path which affords outstanding views of the Sound of Raasay and the 1300-ft (396m) high cliffs that form the coastline to the north of the town. There is a short section on rough ground just before the path reaches The Bile, a remarkable pasture which was formed when the sea-level was at a much higher level than it is today. The route then follows farm tracks before it comes to a junction with another footpath,which winds down through woodland to return to Portree.

Portree is the capital of Skye, and its name (Port an Righ, the King's harbour) dates from 1540, when James V visited. St Columba also landed at Portree, and in 1746 Bonnie Prince Charlie, disguised as a woman, managed to evade his pursuers and sailed from the port, having said farewell to Flora Macdonald at what is now the Royal Hotel.

From the small car park at the end of the shoreline road take the asphalted path by the shore past a picnic table, boathouse and slipway. Go through a gate which bears a notice saying that the land belongs to the Clan Nicholson Trust. Scorrybreac, the ancestral home of

the Clan Mhicneacall, stood here in centuries past.

At the point where the path divides, take the shoreline path past Murdo's Well 'Tobar Mhurchaidh' – named after Murdo Nicholson, an active local member of the clan, who restored it. The path is well provided with seats with views into Loch Portree. The islet of Sgeir Mhór is just offshore – a tiny platform of grass surrounded by rocks. As the path rounds the point **Ⓐ** the magnificent cliffs of Creag Mhór come into view. The path then winds through thick bracken over outcrops of rock and loose stones that become extremely slippery when wet. A gate gives

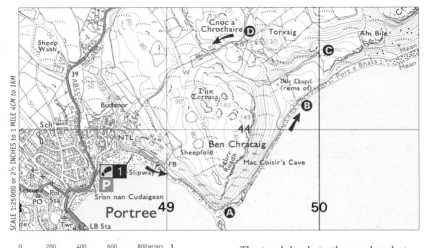

access to the broad grassy shelf of The Bile which slopes gently upwards towards the cliffs.

Turn left at the next fence **B** and follow this up to a gate at the top. Go through the gate and with a fence to the left on to a stile in the corner of the field **C**. Cross the stile and turn left on to a track that climbs up the flank of the hill. There is a stunning view behind you as you near the top.

Portree with the Old Man of Storr

The track leads to the road end at Torvaig **D**. Turn right past the house and then immediately left to descend on a track that passes between two large sheds. After this, the path continues in a straight line by a wall. Granite chippings have been laid to preserve the surface of the path but it has become encroached by saplings. After a stile situated by an ancient kissing-gate, the path goes steeply downhill to come out at new bungalows. Bear left on to the drive to the Cuillin Hills Hotel. With the hotel to the left, descend the drive to return to the starting point. ●

Shieldaig

Start	Shieldaig, Torridon
Distance	2½ miles (4km)
Approximate time	1½ hours
Parking	On the grass in front of the war memorial
Refreshments	Hotel in Shieldaig
Ordnance Survey maps	Landranger 24 (Raasay, Applecross & Loch Torridon) and Outdoor Leisure 8 (The Cuillin & Torridon Hills)

Few places have a more delightful outlook than the village of Shieldaig, which faces west looking towards the Applecross peninsula. The great beauty of the village and its situation has lead to its being featured in countless calendars. The short walk here takes you away from the village on to the headland to the north. The path, which is rough at times, goes round the headland, giving ever-changing views of the Torridon mountains and the coastline of Applecross.

Shieldaig village was founded in 1800 by the Admiralty to serve as a base for training seamen to fight in the war against Napoleon. Incentives were paid to Highland seafarers and fishermen to settle there but at the end of the war the Admiralty's interest ended and the villagers were left to fend for themselves. Fortunately, Loch Torridon had long been famous for its herrings, and fishing was able to sustain the isolated community. At the beginning of this century herring became scarce, but today, with Shieldaig served by good roads running through magnificent mountain landscapes, the village has found a new source of income from tourism. Shieldaig Island, just offshore, is owned by the National Trust for Scotland and is a bird sanctuary, though anyone with a boat may land on its wooded shores.

Camas an Léim and Loch Torridon

From the war memorial, walk down to the school and turn right **A**. Turn right again away from the drive to Rubha Lodge by a rocky knoll. The path is delightfully varied, climbing and falling, to pass through trees to reach an area of smooth grass above a stony beach. Soon after this, Beinn Alligin and Liathach come into view on the right across Loch Torridon.

Keep straight on at a cairn where the path divides **B**: you will return on the path to the left. The path crosses heather and the lovely little beach of Camas an Léim is below to the right. You climb up a short rock staircase and at the top a salmon farm can be seen just offshore. A triangulation pillar is on the hilltop ahead as the path crosses exposed rock. It arrives at Bad-callda, a cottage without road access which relies on a boat for its supplies. Look to the left to see a rocky staircase **C** which takes the path up to another section over moorland. It winds over this for a short distance before descending to another isolated cottage overlooking the rocky Eilean a' Chaoil.

From here the way swings southwards and the path is on the top of the cliffs giving outstanding coastal views both forwards towards Applecross and back across Loch Torridon. This is probably the most memorable part of the walk, and there are many sheltered places where you can pause to enjoy the scenery. The path meanders back to the cairn **B**, and from there you retrace your footsteps to the start. ●

The Armadale Castle Estate

Start	Armadale Castle, south Skye
Distance	2¾ miles (4.5km)
Approximate time	2 hours
Parking	Clan Donald Visitor Centre
Refreshments	Restaurant in former stables at Armadale Castle
Ordnance Survey maps	Landranger 32 (South Skye) and Pathfinder 235, NG 60/70 (Mid Sound of Sleat)

The price of admission to the Clan Donald Visitor Centre gives you the opportunity of exploring the beautiful estate that surrounds it. This short walk not only takes you through the gardens and park but also leads through wild woodland and forest to an all-embracing hilltop viewpoint. The Museum of the Isles in the Visitor Centre illustrates the history of the Clan Donald over 1300 years. The estate requests walkers to close all gates and respect the privacy of residents.

From the car park, walk past the front of the castle (it is up to you whether you visit the visitor centre before or after the walk). Turn right at the far end of the façade and then after about 30 yds (27m) turn left **Ⓐ**, following a sign to the Nature Trails. However, before doing this you may prefer to walk down to the end of the lawn to see the breathtaking views over the Sound of Sleat (pronounced 'slate') to the Knoydart mountains.

Armadale Castle dates from 1815 when the original Macdonald manor house of 1790 was enlarged. However, this mansion was destroyed by fire in 1855, only part of the central block being rebuilt. The remainder was left as an evocative ruin. Dr Johnson and James Boswell stayed with Sir Alexander Macdonald at the old house in September 1773. Although Boswell was related to Sir Alexander, he greatly disliked him, as

did his tenants since he was a cruel and mean landlord in contrast to his elder brother, the previous much-loved laird. Boswell's scathing comments appeared in the first edition of *A Journal of a Tour to the Hebrides* but were expurgated from all later reprints after Sir Alexander had threatened Boswell with a duel.

The path passes beneath specimen trees and by banks of rhododendrons to reach a junction – follow the sign to White Gate. There are good views from this part of the walk, the path being just above the road. On the other side of the road at White Gate a band of rock can be seen stretching into the sea. This is a dyke, an intrusion of the hard volcanic rock dolerite, which has pushed its way through the surrounding gneiss, the most ancient of British bedrocks which characteristically gives sour and infertile soils. Otters are said to

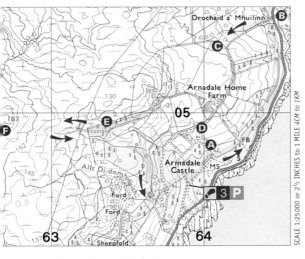

SCALE 1:25 000 or 2½ INCHES to 1 MILE 4CM to 1KM

| 0 | 200 | 400 | 600 | 800 METRES | 1 |
| 0 | 200 | 400 | 600 YARDS | ½ |

KILOMETRES
MILES

enjoy fishing from the dyke when conditions are favourable.

Keep to the upper path when the way divides after White Gate, continuing to enjoy the views seawards. The first part of the walk ends as the path descends almost to the main road at a deer-gate **B**, which gives on to a track climbing steeply uphill. Turn left away from the road to go through the gate and up the track. Until 1823 this was the main highway linking the Sleat peninsula with the rest of Skye. The present road was built to take traffic away from the vicinity of the castle.

The track climbs, at first through trees and then pasture to a gate **C**, where there is a seat and the track swings left. A most pleasant part of the route follows on a grassy track leading to Armadale Farm. Views are screened by a fine row of thorn trees.

At the farm, turn off the main drive to the right **D** to follow a sign pointing to the Hilltop Viewpoint. After about 300 yds (274m) there is a splendid view over the Sound of Sleat with the castle in the foreground to

give scale to the vista. A little further on, the way divides again **E**. Bear right to the Hilltop Viewpoint unless you wish to shorten the walk, in which case make for the Keeper's Cottage.

The way is through a dark stretch of forest for a short distance but then passes through a deer-gate on to open moor. The small pond to the right originally supplied waterpower to drive machinery at the farm. A track – which can be very moist – leads up the hill from here. Follow it for about ½ mile (800m) before leaving it to the right to climb to the Hilltop Viewpoint **F**, where there is an aerial. The panorama is truly amazing in good conditions. To the north you can see Torrin with Beinn na Caillich behind and the Cuillins to the left. To the south it is easy to identify Mallaig and the Sands of Morar.

After passing through the deer-gate and the dark bit of forest, turn right at **E** to the Keeper's Cottage. Note the steel dog runs and turn left towards the castle down Dark Walk, which crosses the road to the farm. At the end of the path turn right to the main drive and the car park. ●

Armadale Castle

Mellon Udrigle

Start	Mellon Udrigle, 3 miles (4.75km) north of Laide and the A832
Distance	3 miles (4.75km)
Approximate time	1¼ hours
Parking	Beach car park at start
Refreshments	None
Ordnance Survey maps	Landranger 19 (Gairloch & Ullapool, Loch Maree) and Pathfinder 110, NG 89/99 (Gruinard Bay)

Mellon Udrigle, with its beach of silver sand backed by dunes, is a crofting township overlooking Gruinard Bay. If Mellon Charles, on the opposite side of the Rubha Mór peninsula, means 'Charles' Little Hill', it is logical that Mellon Udrigle must be 'the Little Hill belonging to Udrigle'. The walk makes a delightful evening stroll with coastal views to the mountains of Coigach and Wester Ross. Allt Loch a' Choire is a tidal loch that attracts many waders, so bird enthusiasts should take their binoculars.

Turn right from the car park in the sand dunes on to the road and after 150 yds (137m) fork left on a track that passes a new bungalow –

Mellon Udrigle

however, do not bear left again just after this on to a surfaced drive that leads to another new bungalow. Keep ahead on a rough track, which soon gives views of the sea. The track crosses moorland on the east side of

an estuary-like loch, Allt Loch a' Choire, where you will usually see curlews and oyster-catchers hunting for crustaceans on the banks of mud and sand. The way becomes grassy as it approaches the shore; there is a cairn on top of the hill ahead, Rubha Beag. When the track finally swings sharply left towards the sea, leave it to the right **A** to climb to the cairn. This proves to be built on the clifftop and is an excellent viewpoint.

Turn right from here to head for another clifftop cairn **B** about ¼ mile (400m) to the south-east, crossing an area riven by deep gullies in the peat. The going is easiest on the seaward side, and the shoreline gives excellent views of the shags and other seabirds on Creag an Eilein

and (if you are fortunate) seals. The second cairn gives views eastwards across the bay over Gruinard Island to Coigach. Beinn Dearg and An Teallach are the dominant mountains further to the south.

Gruinard Island was notorious for being the place where experiments with anthrax bacteria took place during World War II. Many sheep were killed in the experiments, which included dropping bombs containing the deadly germ on the island. A dead sheep floated ashore and infected the herd at Mellon Udrigle. After the war the island was placed out of bounds to everyone, and it was not until 1987 that its soil was cleansed, by means of a spray of formaldehyde mixed with seawater. In 1990 the Ministry of Defence declared Gruinard Island safe, and it was subsequently purchased by its pre-war owners. Nevertheless, it still retains its sinister reputation.

From the second cairn there are also views of Loch Dubh Geodhachan Tharailt and the headland of Meall Leac an Fhaobhair. Make for the latter along the cliffs, passing the north-east shore of the loch. A second loch (Loch Dubh na Maoil) comes into view as you make your way across the heather on a sheep path, which vaguely follows the edge of the cliff.

The hill above the headland **C** is crowned with a cross inscribed 'Ceol na Mara'. From here the horizon is filled with mountains. Turn south-westwards to follow the coastline and passing close to Loch Dubh na Maoil. Head for the clump of conifers which shelter the Old School House on a clear path through the heather. The path meets the end of the road just to the right of this house. Walk back along the road to the car park. ●

The Sanctuary and the Old Man of Storr

Start	About 6½ miles (10.5km) north of Portree, Skye, on the A855, opposite the northern end of Loch Leathan
Distance	3 miles (4.75km)
Approximate time	2½ hours
Parking	Car park at the start
Refreshments	None
Ordnance Survey maps	Landranger 23 (North Skye) and Pathfinder 154, NG 45/55 (Trotternish)

This walk is short but includes a steep climb. It may be extremely wet underfoot in the woodland sections, which come at the beginning and end. For all this the route leads to a place of unique beauty which is worth exploring thoroughly. The descent is enjoyable for the magnificent views facing you until they are blocked off by trees on the lower slopes.

The Sanctuary and the Old Man of Storr

The Old Man of Storr is, after the Cuillins, Skye's most famous landmark. The remarkable pinnacle was formed when the sedimentary rock over which basalt lava had previously flowed, collapsed under its weight. This resulted in some of the most spectacular landslip formations to be found in Britain. The impressive cliffs rising above the Old Man, shelter the surreal hollow known as the Sanctuary, which has more pinnacles and contorted pillars and, as its name implies, is a refuge of tranquillity and beauty.

Take the path on the south-western side of the car park and cross a stile. The path follows a grassy firebreak with electric lines. There is a moist section by a stream, but as compensation there is a view south over the Sound of Raasay with Dùn Caan prominent. The precipitous

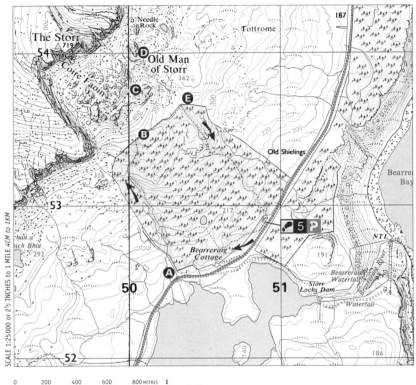

SCALE 1:25000 or 2½ INCHES to 1 MILE 4CM to 1KM

| 0 | 200 | 400 | 600 | 800 METRES | 1 |
| 0 | 200 | 400 | 600 YARDS | ½ | KILOMETRES MILES |

Trotternish cliffs can be seen ahead. The path crests a rise, and suddenly there is a good view to the right of the Old Man of Storr. After another section of wet going, the path comes to a fence. Turn right here **A** on the uphill path with the forest to the right. A stile takes the path to the right of the fence before a burn. Then it follows the stream up to the corner of a fence – this part is very damp. The path becomes extremely steep as it approaches the top of the forest. You may like to pause to enjoy the view back from this point.

After the top fence **B** the weird-shaped pinnacles come into view and look more and more like the set of a science fiction film. The path flattens as it reaches the first group of these and enters the Sanctuary **C**. The

Needle Rock, standing to the left of the Old Man, is easily identifiable though its eye is not immediately obvious. The Old Man is 160ft (49m) high and seems as though it could topple at any moment from its savagely undercut base. Its crumbling rock gives no secure holds and it was not until 1955 that a climber managed to reach the top.

The main path down starts to the left of the Old Man (that is on his northern side) **D**. There is wonderful view as you descend. The lower part of the path, before you reach the forest, has been restored. After a stile **E** keep going straight down, ignoring what looks like a better track to the right. At times this path is very wet, especially where it follows a stream for a time. Eventually, however, it reaches the northern side of the car park from where you began the walk. ●

The Point of Stoer

Start	Stoer lighthouse
Distance	4½ miles (7.25km)
Approximate time	1½ hours
Parking	Lighthouse car park
Refreshments	None
Ordnance Survey maps	Landranger 15 (Loch Assynt) and Pathfinder 72, NC 03/13 (Drumbeg)

This is a beautiful clifftop walk, which will probably stimulate you to explore more of this coastline. The Point of Stoer is at the head of the Assynt peninsula, projecting into the turbulent waters of the North Minch. To the east are Quinag and Ben More and the other summits of Assynt, while the Outer Hebridean islands lie to the west. The clifftop path is a fine viewpoint for spectacular sunsets.

A clear path leads from the car park to the grassy cliffs. The islands of the Outer Hebrides are seen clearly once the top of the cliffs is reached – Lewis is the one closest to the mainland and North Uist has the mountains. Fulmars swoop and dive here over

The wonderful view from Sidhean Mór

the heads of seals, though you need good eyes to see them swimming 300ft (90m) or so below. Keep children and dogs on tight reins here. A stream runs down a gully **Ⓐ** and drops as a waterfall to a stony beach. Cross the gully by diverting a little way inland and then look back for a fine view of the lighthouse with the

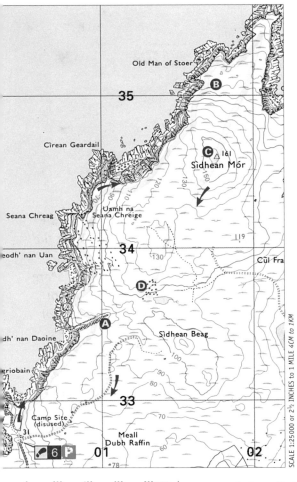

enjoy the challenge of being battered by waves as they climb its perpendicular faces (you will also see them negotiating overhangs). It seems amazing that anyone can find room to stand on the needle-like summit. The path continues to climb to the headland itself, the Point of Stoer, but an even better view is obtained further on when the path swings south and reaches the triangulation pillar on Sidhean Mór **C**.

From here there is a fantastic panorama, and the knowledgeable will be able to display their skill at identifying the summits. The arc ranges from Foinaven and Arkle to the left, through the Assynt peaks to the east with the sharp peaks of Quinag distinctive, round to the Coigach Mountains to the right. Then you can turn seawards to try to name the grand array of islands.

From the triangulation pillar make for a point midway between the lighthouse and the radio mast (which is not shown on the map). Skirt round the right-hand edge of a peaty basin; the gully crossed earlier can be seen from here. Climb the hill **D** on the other side of the basin; there is a lochan to the left and a cairn to the right while straight ahead is the track from the radio mast to the lighthouse. Join this to return to the car park, continuing to enjoy grand views ahead and to the left.

impressive cliffs, composed of great slabs of Torridonian sandstone, in the foreground. Cormorants and shags enjoy fishing from the rock platforms at the base of the cliffs.

Soon the Old Man of Stoer comes into view ahead **B**. It is 220ft (67m) high and before the lighthouse was built was a famous landmark to seamen. Rob Donn Mackay wrote of it in verse, and the rock probably gave its name to the peninsula since Stoer is derived from the Norse word *staurr*, meaning a stake. It is a popular venue for rock-climbers who

Ardheslaig on the Applecross Peninsula

Start	Kenmore, 8 miles (12.75km) from Shieldaig
Distance	4½ miles (7.25km)
Approximate time	2½ hours
Parking	At Kenmore, where the road to the village leaves the main road
Refreshments	Tea and coffee at Ardheslaig
Ordnance Survey maps	Landranger 24 (Applecross & Raasay) and Pathfinder 155, NG 65/75 (Arinacrinachd)

This short walk uses road and footpath in almost equal measure in a figure-of-eight route that gives some glorious vistas of Torridon. Applecross is notorious for the mountain road that leads to the village, but Kenmore, the starting point here, is to the north of Applecross and easily reached via the coastal road from Shieldaig. This, though tortuous and narrow, also provides views of magnificent scenery.

Until the early 1970s the only motor road to Applecross was via the Bealach na Bà, the Pass of the Cattle, a route which was notorious for its difficulty. Kenmore is a hamlet on the seaward side of the modern coastal road. Park in the wide space by the Kenmore turning and turn left to

Ardheslaig

walk along the road with the sea to the left. Climb a hill to a passing-place that bears a bridleway notice on its sign. Leave the road here **Ⓐ** and go on to a footpath that follows electric lines down to a wooden footbridge. After crossing this there is a short section of path through high heather and bracken, which will leave trousers damp if there has been recent rain. The path has an ancient feel to it and seems haunted by the spirits of the drovers and tinkers who used it a century or more before the new road was built. Croic-bheinn is the fine mountain ahead as you climb with the stream to the right.

Pause before you reach the summit of the path to look back over Kenmore with its white cottages and the Applecross coastline beyond. The path turns northwards to give a view of Loch na Creige and later curves right to enter a broad defile. This leads up to its summit **B** where, dramatically, Ardheslaig is revealed below. The picture of the fishing village on Loch Beag, with Loch Torridon and the mountains beyond, is one of the classic views of the North-west Highlands.

Continue along the path, and when it divides, take the right fork to climb up to the road past a redundant telephone pole.

Turn left on to the road **C** and enjoy the easy descent to Ardheslaig, with the magnificent scenery of the Torridon mountains facing you.

Ardheslaig takes its name from the Norse word meaning 'Hazel Bay'. It was probably strategically important to Viking settlers as it guarded the entrances to lochs Torridon and Shieldaig. Viking rule lasted in the west of Scotland from around AD 400 until 1266, when Norway relinquished its hold on the Scottish islands and parts of the mainland after the Battle of Largs. Subsequently the Torridon district was owned by the Lords of the Isles.

The first house in the village is Innis Mhór. Cross the bridge here **D** to the left of the road and turn left on to the footpath, which, as before, follows the course of the old road.

The grassy path climbs up to the road again though you may like to wander a little way to the right of it to find the best viewpoints of the Torridon landscape from the rocky knolls to seaward. The footpath continues to climb and passes what looks like a roadside gravestone. Just after this there is a short scramble at the end of the path up to the crash barriers. Once back on the road **E**, the route-finding is easy. Walk past Loch na Creige – the 'the Loch of the Crag' – where there is another good view of Croic-bheinn with its steep west-facing cliff – and follow the road for another 20 minutes or so to return to the starting point at Kenmore. ●

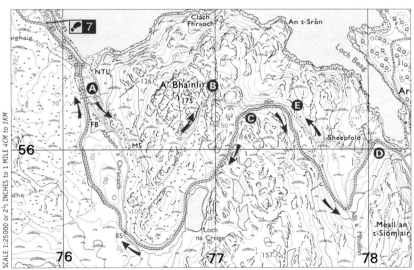

Rubha Hunish

Start	At the telephone-box about ½ mile (800m) west of the Duntulm Hotel, Duntulm, north Skye
Distance	4½ miles (7.25km)
Approximate time	3 hours
Parking	At start
Refreshments	Hotel in Duntulm
Ordnance Survey maps	Landranger 23 (North Skye) and Pathfinder 127, NG 37/47 (Rubha Hunish)

The most northerly point of Skye is Rubha Hunish, the Point of the Bear, a peninsula which, when viewed from the towering cliffs, seems utterly inaccessible. However, a fearsome-looking path descends the cliffs and leads to a place of unique beauty. Those who suffer from vertigo should not attempt it but be content with a walk which takes you over moorland to the top of 300-ft (100m) high cliffs.

Park by the telephone-box and take the public footpath through the gate to pass the sheep-pens. The path crosses an earth bank and then joins a maze of sheep-tracks. Keep heading towards the sea above low ground to the left – the various wayward tracks soon merge to form a recognisable path going straight ahead towards the sea on a low escarpment.

Walk past the upper crofts of the abandoned township of Erisco **Ⓐ**, unusual in once having cottages built along a straight line, grass-covered

The cliffs overlooking Hunish

mounds betraying their locations. The path hugs the side of the hill as it approaches a stile over a fence, following a dyke for the last few yards. This is a good place for a view of the derelict crofts of Erisco with Tulm Island and Duntulm Castle in the distance. The path climbs steadily but fades as it reaches the top of the high ground **Ⓑ**. Here you face a defile with rocky ground rising on both sides. If the weather has been dry you will find it relatively easy to make your way along the defile but in moist conditions keep above the boggy ground and go along the rocky ridge to the right. However, you will have to cross the valley at its seaward end to reach the pointed rock that marks the beginning of the 300-ft (100m) descent to Rubha Hunish **Ⓒ** The best views of the peninsula and the islands of the Outer Hebrides are seen from the path beyond the coastguard station to the right.

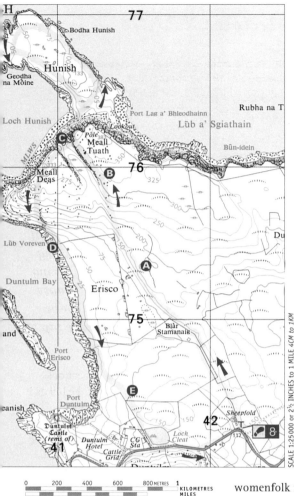

H

Bodha Hunish

77

Hunish

Geodha na Mòine

Loch Hunish

Port Lag a' Bhleodhainn

Rubha na T

C

Pòle
Meall
Tuath

Lookout

Lùb a' Sgiathain

Bùn-idein

Meall
Deas

B

76

Lùb Voreven

D

A

Du

Duntulm Bay

Erisco

75

and

Blàr
Stamanail

Port
Erisco

E

Port
Duntulm

Sheepfold

42

eanish

Duntulm
Castle
(rems of)

Duntulm
Hotel

CG
Sta

Loch
Cleat

Cattle
Grid

41

SCALE 1:25000 or 2½ INCHES to 1 MILE 4CM to 1KM

0	200	400	600	800 METRES	1
					KILOMETRES
					MILES
0	200	400	600 YARDS	½	

surface to cast its limpid eyes on you.

Return up the path to the top of the cliffs and take the path south-westwards, following the cliff-edge. You may be able to follow a sheep-track for part of the way but most of the time will be over springy heather. It is hard to become lost with the sea constantly to the right. At length you will drop down to a fence, which is crossed by means of a stile made from fish-boxes **D**. From here a path follows the shore, threading through the pock-marked volcanic rocks, with Duntulm Castle ahead. This was a stronghold of the Macdonalds before they moved south to Armadale, Edinburgh and London. Their womenfolk made a garden with soil brought from seven kingdoms and, looking at the crumbling walls today, it is hard to imagine the great feast given by Donald of the Wars, when fifty maidens danced for him.

As you approach the end of Tulm Island, begin to head away from the sea towards a radio mast on the skyline. Go through a metal gate **E** by the corner of a wall and then keep the wall to the right. The chimneys of the former coastguard cottages can be seen ahead. Go through two more gates – the first is to the right – to follow a track past the cottages to the road. Turn left to walk back to the start, past Loch Cleat. ●

The way down from the rock looks formidable but is less terrifying once you have negotiated the rocky staircase at the start. Rubha Hunish is a place of great beauty, with plenty of rock pools full of clearest seawater where you can cool off if you have been fortunate enough to come here on a hot summer's day. From the bottom you can look up at the gigantic basalt columns of the cliff face. Fulmars, shags, gannets and many other seabirds fly from the cliffs and shore and, if you sit quietly to watch, an inquisitive seal may

The Quiraing

Start	From the summit of the pass on the Uig–Staffin road 3 miles (4.75km) west of Staffin, north Skye
Distance	4½ miles (7.25km)
Approximate time	3 hours
Parking	Layby at top of the pass
Refreshments	None
Ordnance Survey maps	Landranger 23 (North Skye) and Pathfinders 127, NG 37/47 (Rubha Hunish) and 138, NG 46/56 (Staffin)

The crags and pinnacles of the Quiraing are a spectacular feature of the scenery of North Skye, and most visitors to the island drive over the pass to view them from the road. However, only a handful take the trouble to explore the lovely path that leads through the landslip beneath its famous features – the Prison, the Needle and the Table. The path to the latter has become badly eroded but this route allows a magnificent view of it from above on the return leg. It would be foolish to attempt this walk in mist.

In high summer you may have to be an early bird to find a place in the layby at the top of the pass, though there are more places to park off the road a little closer to Uig. From the layby, cross the road to join the path leading towards the enticing pinnacles and rock faces. As you climb, look across the Sound of Raasay to the mountains of the Applecross peninsula – the summit of the pass is at 817ft (249m) so you already enjoy an eagle's-eye view of the beautiful landscape. In the light of a fine summer morning Raasay looks as though it is afloat in a sea of mist. Hands have to be used to cross a gully early in this part of the walk.

After about 20 minutes, the path crosses a second stone-filled gully and swings round a buttress. After this, the Prison comes into view to the right, an enormous sheer-sided slab of rock, which merits its name. At the end of the Ice Age a bed of solidified lava about 1000ft (300m) thick, broke away and began to slip

The Table, Quiraing, Skye

towards the sea, creating the weird landscape here. The path bears left to go below the sheer face of the Prison, with the Needle the pinnacle to the left. At the col **Ⓐ** below the Prison there is a cairn, which marks where a path leads up to the Table. This has become badly eroded and is not recommended, though once cattle were driven up the steep, grassy slope to be concealed in the Table. 'Quiraing' derives from the Norse word meaning 'crooked enclosure', and it was written that 3,000 head of cattle could be concealed here from piratical raiders.

Continue on the path northwards from **Ⓐ**, crossing an old fence and passing below an overhanging rock to find a different scene suddenly unveiled. The new, verdant landscape has a lochan with another group of pinnacles beyond. Continue past the lochan, walking towards the col and keeping the pinnacles of Leac nan Fionn to the right. After the wall at the top of the col, bear left **Ⓑ** to reach a cairn and continue bearing left as you climb so that by the end of the steep haul you have turned to head southwards. The last part of the climb is up the side of a deep gully. There are wonderful views down to the Table as you approach the cairn at the summit **Ⓒ**. You will probably have already paused several

times on the way up to enjoy the views to the north and east but the Table is the climax of this walk and its smooth grass about 150ft (137m) below makes a wonderful foreground for photographs.

The final part of the walk follows the top of the cliffs. The descent is gradual but pathless so it is wise to swing slightly westwards away from the edge near the end **Ⓓ** to avoid descending too precipitously to rejoin the outward path close to the road. ●

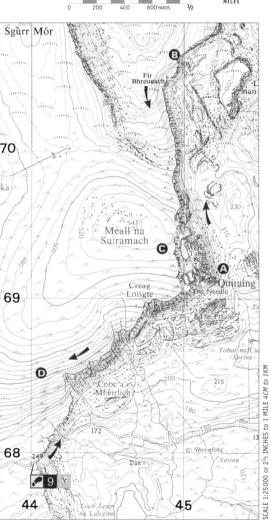

The Point of Sleat

Start	At the end of the public road, Aird of Sleat, south Skye
Distance	5 miles (8km)
Approximate time	4 hours
Parking	Car park at start
Refreshments	None
Ordnance Survey maps	Landranger 32 (South Skye) and Pathfinder 234, NG 50 (Aird of Sleat)

A good moorland track takes you to Acairseid an Rubha, a tiny fishing inlet where you can climb to the headland and enjoy views to Eigg and Rum as well as along the rugged coastline of Sleat. Continue from here across somewhat damp ground to reach the lighthouse on the Point of Sleat, the southernmost tip of Skye and an even better viewpoint, looking across to Morar, Moidart, Ardnamurchan, Coll and Tiree, as well as to the Cuillin Hills to the north-east.

Sleat is known as 'the Garden of Skye', and certainly as you drive past the parkland of Armadale with its fine trees it seems a different country to the rest of the island. However, further to the south-west the landscape changes again, the trees are forgotten, and you are returned to the land of rock and water.

The starting point for this walk is at the end of the road in Aird of Sleat, by the former church. Go through the gate to a good track through a heathery, hummocky landscape, which climbs steadily. The top of the first rise reveals a delightful Hebridean landscape with Rum and Eigg prominent. The track dips down from here but soon rises again, and this reveals the shore ahead. Look back from here and you have a grand vista of the mountains of Morar and Moidart to the south-east across the Sound of Sleat. After a gate the way

lies along a path by a steep-sided burn. The path is smoother than the track used previously and passes a pretty creekside cottage with a

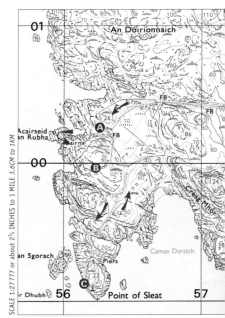

The Point of Sleat, Skye

garden filled with daffodils in spring to reach a gate **Ⓐ**.

Go through the gate and walk past a cottage on the quay to scramble up Acairseid an Rubha, a headland with three tall cairns, which gives wonderful coastal and island views. Many walkers are happy to have reached this objective, but having come this far it is a shame not to take a little more time to reach the Point of Sleat, an even finer viewpoint.

Return past the quayside cottage towards **Ⓐ** but turn to the right immediately before the bridge over the small burn. Climb up the rocky defile, which soon becomes a path following a fence to the left. From the corner of the fence **Ⓑ** keep ahead, passing a delightful rocky cove to the right. The path swings eastwards along the top of a series of heather-covered hillocks and then passes through a boggy defile. This leads to another beautiful bay fringed by smooth turf – the ideal place for a picnic. The path swings right before reaching it to run parallel to the shore. It then climbs to the top of a hill, revealing the lighthouse ahead.

The path through the heather south-westwards is now well defined and descends the left side of a col to reach concrete steps (the lower ones are eroded). A stone causeway then leads through a rocky ravine to the storm beach, which links the point to the mainland. The abundance of seaweed as a natural manure makes the grass grow richly here, and you will even find stinging nettles as well. The beach is sandy at low tide. From a wooden hut, walk up more steps to reach the unmanned lighthouse **Ⓒ**. The higher ground immediately above the lighthouse gives magnificent panoramas westwards over Rum to North and South Uist, southwards to Moidart and beyond, and eastwards to Lochaber. The shape of Ben Nevis may be picked out to the south-east.

The return has to be made using the same route, but the views are just as enjoyable going in this direction. ●

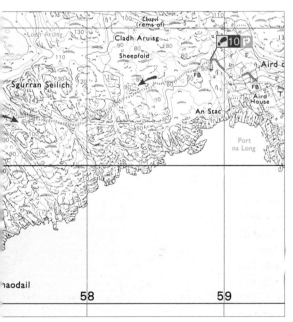

The Fairy Lochs from Shieldaig

Start	Approaching Shieldaig on the B8056 to Badachro, about 1 mile (1.5km) west of its junction with the A832
Distance	5 miles (8km)
Approximate time	2½ hours
Parking	On verge at the start
Refreshments	Shieldaig Lodge Hotel
Ordnance Survey maps	Landranger 19 (Gairloch & Ullapool, Loch Maree) and Outdoor Leisure 8 (The Cuillin & Torridon Hills)

Some people may feel that it is morbid to visit the remote site of a wartime tragedy, though most who see the remains of the Liberator, which crashed in 1945, will find it a poignant memorial to the young airmen who lost their lives. There is more to the walk than this, and lovers of wild countryside, if they have the relevant map, may like to continue up the Braigh Horrisdale a further 5 miles (8km) or so to the lovely Loch a' Bhealaich. Note that the going can be very wet on this walk.

The memorial at the Fairy Lochs

A mile (1.5km) or so after leaving the A832, the Badachro road (B8056) comes to a track on the left about 100 yds (91m) before the Shieldaig Lodge Hotel. There is room to park two or three cars on the verge of the road here. Climb the track past farm buildings and keep ahead, when another track goes off to the right to a cottage hidden amongst trees.

The track climbs up Glac Sieldaig (*glac* meaning 'hollow' and *Sieldaig* being the Gaelic spelling of 'Shieldaig', from the Norse for 'herring bay'). It is sometimes rough and wet underfoot and you pass a cairn on the right **A**, which is opposite the point where the return path rejoins the track. Keep on the track, which becomes narrower as it climbs through trees by a stream. In about 20 minutes you will reach a beautiful lochan, overlooked by a small crag, which is a good viewpoint over Loch Gairloch. Walk a little further and you will come to Loch Braigh Horrisdale. A steeply inclined bridge takes the track over a ravine on its eastern shore **B**. You can use the bridge to reach a sandy beach, ideal for picnics. However, the route does not cross the bridge but follows the path that leaves just before it to follow a burn upstream.

The path is tortuous, short climbs being followed by stretches over boggy ground where cairns mark the way. Soon the path reaches a lochan with water-lilies **C** – this is the first of the Lochan Sgeireach, better known as the Fairy Lochs. The scene looks idyllic at first but as you progress along the path you will note alien features: there is an aero-engine on an island at the end of the loch, and a scattering of burned aluminium on the shore beneath a little eminence shows where most of the wreckage of the aircraft fell.

The memorial plaque is positioned on the face of a small cliff at the end of the loch, which was hit by the Liberator on 13 June 1945, the fifteen crew and passengers all being killed. The aircraft was on its journey back to the United States when it became lost and crashed here in poor visibility. The wreckage serves as a memorial to the dead and should not

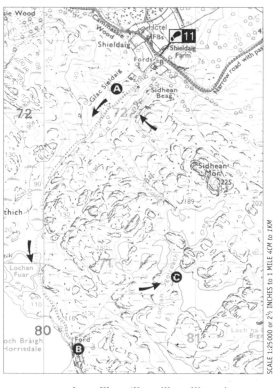

SCALE 1:25000 or 2½ INCHES to 1 MILE 4CM to 1KM

| 0 | 200 | 400 | 600 | 800 METRES | 1 |
| 0 | 200 | 400 | 600 YARDS | ½ | KILOMETRES / MILES |

be touched. As the plaque says, having listed the names and ages of those who died: 'This site is their last resting place. Please treat with respect and take only memories'. Beneath the plaque there is a poignant memorial made from pieces of the wreckage. From here continue along the path with the loch to the left, climbing to reach a ridge, where another loch is revealed to the right.

A little further and a wonderful view opens up over Loch Gairloch with the Outer Isles in the distance. You will continue to enjoy these views as you descend – but do not become distracted since the path drops steeply at times and is often muddy. All too soon the path rejoins the track **A**, and a return is soon made to the starting point. ●

Flowerdale Waterfalls, Gairloch

Start	Gairloch Golf Club, at the south end of Charlestown village (A832)
Distance	5 miles (8km); shorter walk 3 miles (4.75km)
Approximate time	3½ hours; shorter walk 2½ hours
Parking	Public car park at start
Refreshments	Teas and snacks at the golf club, pub on main road opposite pier
Ordnance Survey maps	Landranger 19 (Gairloch & Ullapool, Loch Maree) and Pathfinder 129, NG 87/97 (Loch Maree North)

The time quoted above for this walk may seem excessive, and undoubtedly it would be if walkers followed the simple 'there and back' route to the picturesque waterfalls. However, the return suggested here is over pathless hillside where the going is rough. In compensation, the views over Gairloch to Skye and the Outer Hebrides are outstanding.

From the car park next to the Gairloch Golf Club, take the path to the beach between the clubhouse and the wall of the Old Burial Ground. Turn left to walk along the wide, sandy beach to An Dùn at its southern end. Climb the steps here to follow the signpost to Gairloch Pier. Bear left when this path divides to reach the top of the hill **Ⓐ**. There are wonderful views from here in almost every direction. Follow the path

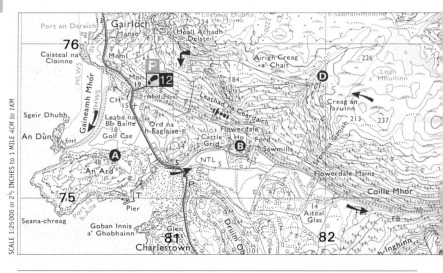

down by the side of a fence and bear right when it divides to descend by a shellfish-processing shed to the quay.

Fishing and tourism are the two important industries at Gairloch today (*gair* means 'short'). It used to be famous for its boatyard, run by one Roderick Mackenzie, whose reputation was based on the pact he had once made with a mermaid. He managed to catch her by the hair and would only agree to let her go when she promised that none of the boats he built would ever sink.

At the landward end of the quay, cross straight over the main road on to the road to Flowerdale House and pass the Old Inn on the right. There are specimen trees to the left, some about 80ft (24m) tall, and a lake to the right as you walk down the drive. Flowerdale Forest takes its name from this estate – some consider it to be the most beautiful mountain area in Scotland. The drive reaches a T-junction **B** after passing the lovely house built by Sir Alexander Mackenzie in 1738. In 1746 a British warship shot a cannonball into the seaward gable of the building. The ship had been sent to the north-west to mete out reprisals to highlanders for supporting Bonnie Prince Charlie. The action was totally unjust in this case since the Mackenzies had taken no side in the conflict. The original home of the head of the Mackenzie clan – 'An Tigh Dige' meaning 'the moated house' – was built in 1494 and stood just below Flowerdale House, though nothing survives of it today. In the potato famine of the mid-19th century the Dowager Lady Mackenzie attempted to ease local hardship by having 'destitution roads' made, thus giving employment to many local men.

To return to the car park from point **B**, *walk 20 yds (18m) past the entrance gate to the house and then turn right through an opening, which leads into woodland to the right of the house. There is an overgrown water garden to the left, and the path goes beneath fine lime trees. Ignore a track leading to the left but bear right to climb to another track by a Flowerdale Waterfall signboard. Turn left on to this path through beautiful woodland and when you come to a collapsed bridge detour left to cross the burn and enter a wide expanse of clear ground between forestry plantings. Follow the path through this clearing to the new cemetery. Turn left to a gate and go through this to walk the short distance to the main road and the car park.*

After passing the house, turn right and follow the sign to Flowerdale Waterfall. A notice at a gate tells how the area around the waterfall has been replanted with native species of trees in an attempt to re-create the ancient forest.

The surfaced road ends at a farm. The timber has been harvested here,

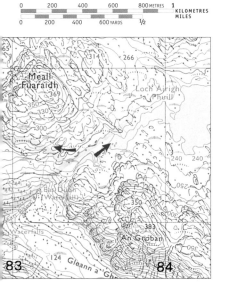

Flowerdale, Gairloch

and though there is some evidence of replanting the hillside is barren. The track leads to a bridge **C** and the two lower falls. The bridge was built in 1993 by the Royal Engineers. Cross the bridge if you wish to view these falls closely, otherwise take the path that leaves the track before the bridge to follow the northern bank of the Easan Bàna. The path climbs steeply to reach the upper waterfalls and a deer-fence. In early summer the damp ground which surrounds the stream abounds in orchids. Is this the reason for the name of the district? There are high steps over the deer-fence, and after these the path continues by the stream to reach Loch Airigh a' Phuill, set amongst low and desolate hills.

Having experienced the flavour of this landscape, return by the stream and then, when it comes into sight, head for a large boulder perched on a rocky platform. From here you can see the deer-fence that surrounds the Flowerdale demesne. Make for this fence and follow its switchback course westwards. The going is tough over the heather so progress will be slow. To compensate, the views onward become increasingly spectacular. They are at their best when the fence drops away steeply from the height of Creag an Iaruinn, and from here you can see Flowerdale House and its wooded policies as well as the golf-course, pier and beach. Navigation through the heather and gorse patches here is largely a matter of instinct but you should be able to reach Allt Loch a' Mhuillinn, the stream draining from the loch, which provides the house with its water. This is crossed by stepping-stones **D** close to a skeletal pine tree and formidable banks of gorse.

From this point there is a more obvious path, which follows an older deer-fence. This leads through a narrow, rocky pass by the site of an old croft. The final part of the route is a steep descent by the fence. The going here is difficult, but pause occasionally to enjoy the wonderful all-round views. At the bottom, go through a gate in the deer-fence, and then cross a wide expanse of open ground close to the top wall of the new cemetery. Go through the gate to the right to reach the main road and the car park. ●

Fairy Pools and Coire na Creiche

Start	Picnic site in Glen Brittle Forest, Skye
Distance	5½ miles (8.75km)
Approximate time	3½ hours
Parking	Car park at picnic site
Refreshments	None
Ordnance Survey maps	Landranger 32 (South Skye) and Outdoor Leisure 8 (The Cuillin & Torridon Hills)

There can be few more apt names than the one given to the series of pools and waterfalls on the Allt Coir' a' Tairneilear and, further down, the Allt Coir' a' Mhadaidh. These two streams flow from the rocky wastes of the Cuillin into the Coire na Creiche to form the River Brittle and in doing so provide bathing-places for Skye's 'Little People'. The outward part of the walk is steep and all of it is over rough, and often wet, ground.

Coire na Creiche may be translated as 'Corrie of the Spoils', the 'spoils' in this case meaning rustled cattle for in the days of clan warfare this was where stolen cattle were often concealed. In 1601 a savage battle took place here when the Macdonalds defeated the Macleods, much to the anger of James VI, who was attempting to control clan warfare in

Fairy Pools, Skye

SCALE 1:25 000 or 2½ INCHES to 1 MILE 4CM to 1KM

0	200	400	600	800 METRES	1
0	200	400	600 YARDS	½	

KILOMETRES
MILES

order to impress Elizabeth I with his influence over the unruly chieftains. The Cuillins are an ever-present feature of this walk though only a few of the twenty-four jagged peaks in the range are visible. Although it has now been established that they got their name from a Norse word meaning the keel of a boat, the earlier explanation that Cuillin derives from the Gaelic for a leaf of sea-holly seems more appropriate. The

mountains we see today once formed a great plateau which rose to a height of some 16,000ft (4877m).

From the car park and picnic place in Glen Brittle Forest, turn left and walk down the road, which soon drops round two sharp bends. After these, leave the road to the left **A** to follow the electricity line downhill. At the second pole, turn left on to a path by the edge of the forest and cross a stream just below a small waterfall. This may call for a jump and a long stride if the water is high. Sgùrr an Fheadain, 2257ft (688m), is

the watershed to see the view from the Bealach a' Mhaim ('Pass of the Gentle Hill') to Loch Sligachan.

Turn right at the cairn **B** on to a path marked by a series of mini-cairns. This heads south towards the main heights of the Cuillin, but it is well worth stopping occasionally to look back. Loch Harport will be seen to the left. The path is good, mainly on grass, except where it crosses scree. At length it comes to the main stream flowing into Coire na Creiche, the Allt Coir' a' Tairneilear.

Turn right **C** on to the path that follows the northern bank of the stream, which as it descends becomes steadily more spectacular. There are waterfalls and deep pools whose blue waters look tempting on a hot day, though few would chance a swim if the burn is in spate. The force of the water has etched out remarkable swirl-holes, and rowan trees stand by many of the waterfalls. When you look back towards the mountains, a prominent feature is Waterpipe Gully on Sgùrr an Fheadain, which seems to have split the peak in half. The stark rock looks forbidding but is loved by climbers for its secure and stable holds.

The waterfalls and the ravines become steadily more impressive as the stream grows and in places there are rusty stains on the bedrock where salts of iron have been dissolved by the torrent. A little way beyond the last of the ravines, the path climbs above the stream **D** and, soon after this, swings northwards to leave its banks to head back to the forest. It crosses two quite substantial tributary burns before it comes to the electricity poles again. Follow the path beneath the electricity cables to the road and turn right to return to the starting point. ●

the dominant feature with its pyramid-shaped peak distinctive at the head of the corrie. The path is spread wide as it comes to boggy ground near the top corner of the forest and it can be seen far ahead, climbing to the top of a ridge.

Continue to follow the path until you come to twin cairns: a big one on the left and a smaller one to the right. It will have taken you about an hour to reach this point. Follow the path for another 150 yds (137m) to a cairn by a lochan **B**. You may like to walk a little distance beyond the lochan to

Ramasaig, Lorgill and the Hoe

Start	Ramasaig, at the end of the road off the B884 from Glendale, Skye
Distance	5 miles (8km)
Approximate time	3 hours
Parking	Spaces to park at the end of the lane (do not impede farming activity)
Refreshments	None
Ordnance Survey maps	Landranger 23 (North Skye) and Pathfinder 152, NG 14/15 (Dunvegan Head & Moonen Bay)

The outward part of the walk is easy going on a good track and leads to Lorgill, once a well-populated crofting village. The return is more energetic and begins with a climb up the steep, grassy slope to the top of the cliff. The way then follows the edge of the cliffs below the Hoe, and there are magnificent coastal views. Note that dogs are not allowed on this route.

The drive to Ramasaig is an enjoyable part of the excursion, with fine coastal views from the road. Walk past the sheep-pens at the end of the road, cross the bridge and go through a kissing-gate to the left of a metal gate. The track passes to the right of a cowshed and soon leaves the Ramasaig pastures. Cross a ford with a small waterfall just above it. After this the track climbs to cross a small

Lorgill Bay, Skye

bealach. Look back from here for a glorious view across Moonen Bay to the Neist lighthouse. The cliffs of Waterstein Head, almost 1,000ft (305m) high, are also well seen. A little further on, the waterfalls of Gleann a' Phuill and An Dubh Loch can be seen to the left with Macleod's Tables beyond. The track passes through a gate and bends to the left past a long-abandoned croft. Leave the track here **A** and take the grassy path descending through pastureland to cross a fence close to a post.

The walking is excellent, over springy turf, past the remains of more cottages **B**. Lorgill thrived until 1830 when its people were evicted from their homes and shipped to Nova Scotia to make way for sheep.

You will reach the shore at Lorgill Bay about an hour after starting from

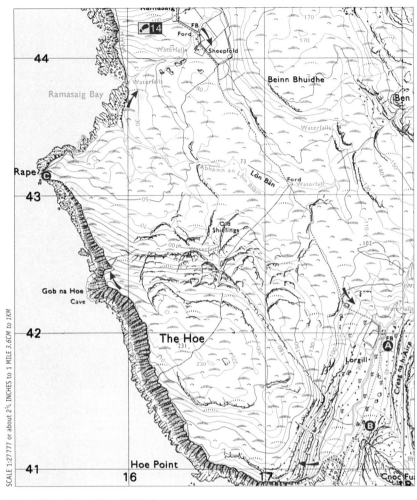

SCALE 1:27 777 or about 2¼ INCHES to 1 MILE 3.6CM to 1KM

Ramasaig. The remains of an old steel lifeboat lie on the beach – one can only wonder at how it came here.

If conditions are dry there is no difficulty in climbing the steep heather-covered slopes to reach the top of the cliffs. However, if the grass is damp it is wiser to start the climb further inland, a little way above the fence crossed earlier. Either way, once you have reached the top of the cliffs make for Hoe Point, following the fence that guards the clifftop. This ends as the cliffs reach their highest

point and a wall strikes inland. Cross the wall and continue, taking care to avoid the cliff-edge but enjoying the breathtaking coastal scenery. Look back occasionally as well for views south-eastwards to the Cuillins.

The headland of Hoe Rape **C** provides the best views of Ramasaig Bay – if there has been recent rain you will see the waterfall where the Moonen Burn plunges to the sea. Ramasaig itself is also clearly visible, and scenically this part of the route provides a fitting finale. When you get to the point where the Ramasaig burn meets the sea, follow the stream back to the starting point. ●

Coire Làgan and Eas Mór

Start	Glen Brittle, Skye
Distance	5½ miles (8.75km)
Approximate time	4½ hours
Parking	Car park at start
Refreshments	None
Ordnance Survey maps	Landranger 32 (South Skye) and Outdoor Leisure 8 (The Cuillin & Torridon Hills)

This walk begins with a demanding climb of over 1800ft (550m) to reach a lochan in one of the most spectacular of the Cuillin corries. It is usually stressed that this is as far as ordinary walkers should venture and, looking at the scree slopes and nearly vertical crags that face you from this point, this advice seems obvious. There is a fascination in sitting beside the lochan and watching climbers struggling up the screes and rock-faces. The return is a gentle descent down the hillside past Eas Mór, a waterfall in a mountainous setting.

From the lochside car park, walk to the campsite and go through the gate on the right, past the toilet block to a stile. Go over this and carry on up a path that climbs steeply and crosses a Land Rover track. Keep ahead after this **A** when a path leaves to the right and crosses the stream. The

footpath is being restored by the Skye and Lochalsh Footpath Initiative. It is sobering to think how badly eroded it would have become without their aid. An information board close to the car park tells of their work in repairing footpaths and how those using them can help in their preservation.

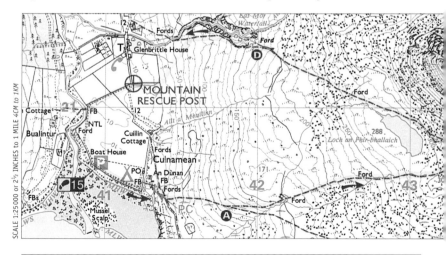

The path climbs steadily into Coire Làgan with Sròn na Cìche the jagged ridge to the right. Loch an Fhirbhaillach is to the left. After about an hour's climbing, a path goes to the left by a pointed rock. Just above this there are twin cairns by the path, and another path leaves to the left **B**, which is used for the return leg. After this the going gradually becomes more difficult. The worst part is when the path climbs through a rocky crevasse, but once this is overcome you soon reach the lochan at the heart of the Coire Làgan **C**. This is an awesome place. Cliffs 1000ft (300m) or so high vanish into the clouds, and minuscule figures can be seen struggling valiantly up sloping ledges beneath them. Others enjoy exhilarating runs down the scree slopes. The best-known of these is the Great Stone Chute to the right, falling from Sgurr Alasdair, at 3257ft (993m) the highest of the Cuillin summits. This was named after Alexander Nicholson who, in 1873, was the first man to climb it. The views seaward to Rum and the islands of the Outer Hebrides are

Eas Mór

equally memorable, and it is easy to spend an hour or so in this magical place exploring and taking pictures.

When it is time to move on, return down the rocky staircase in the crevasse and walk back to the twin cairns **B**. Turn right here to leave the main path on to one that traverses the hillside, giving fine views out to sea. It drops down to the shore of Loch an Fhir-bhaillach and will probably be muddy for much of the way. It continues to be moist beyond the loch but remains distinct. At length you will hear the sound of the waterfall, Eas Mór **D**.

You will find that the best view of the waterfall is from a grassy ledge reached after passing a group of rowan trees. The path follows the stream down. However, when you see a wall at the top of the fields, turn left away from Glen Brittle House to walk by the top wall to reach a gap between two fences, which leads down to the Mountain Rescue Post. This is an unmanned rallying point and store for equipment. Turn left on to the road here to return to the Glen Brittle car park. ●

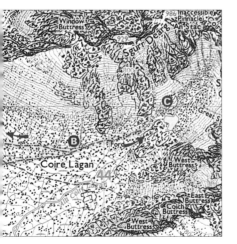

Coire Mhic Fhearchair

Start	Car park at head of Glen Torridon
Distance	8 miles (12.9km)
Approximate time	5 hours
Parking	At start
Refreshments	None
Ordnance Survey maps	Landranger 25 (Glen Carron) and 19 (Gairloch & Ullapool, Loch Maree), and Outdoor Leisure 8 (Cuillin & Torridon Hills)

This walk takes you deep into the heart of the Torridon wilderness to visit one of Scotland's most spectacular mountain corries. Coire Mhic Fhearchair (pronounced 'corrie vik erracher') is ringed by impressive cliffs of sandstone and quartzite, towering above the dark waters of a tranquil lochan. The walk is long but enjoys gentle gradients and a well-made path for most of the way. Choose a fine summer's day when the hilltops are clear of cloud as the stunning scenery is the main attraction.

The walk begins beside the bridge immediately east of the Glen Torridon car park, where a good path, signposted 'Public Footpath to Coire Mhic Fhearchair and Coire Mhic Nobuil', climbs steadily toward Coire Dubh Mór, which is the deep hollow between Beinn Eighe and Liathach, two of the finest mountains in Scotland. After about 40 minutes of climbing, the path levels out and crosses the Allt a' Choire Dhuibh Mhóir at a line of large stepping-stones **Ⓐ**. Up ahead you can see Beinn Dearg, while on the left the craggy northern face of Liathach comes into view. Another 15 minutes beyond the stepping-stones the path descends slightly and passes a small, reedy lochan on the right. Immediately after the lochan, bear right at a junction that is marked by a large cairn **Ⓑ**.

The route now crosses a broad shelf of bare Torridonian sandstone to another large cairn, then contours around the foot of Sàil Mhór on a path that has recently been rebuilt by the NTS (ignore the old, eroded path that you can see a little further down the hillside). You are now heading towards the remote heart of Flowerdale Forest, with the broad, lochan-studded wilderness of Strath Lungard framed between the conical peak of Beinn an Eoin on the left, and the steep escarpment of Beinn a' Chearcaill on the right, with a glimpse of Loch Maree visible in the distance.

As the path continues around the northern flank of Sàil Mhór it becomes rougher and less well defined, but the route is still obvious – a rising traverse around to your right. About 40 or 50 minutes after leaving the cairns at **Ⓑ** you will see

SCALE 1:25000 or 2½ INCHES to 1 MILE 4CM to 1KM

| 0 | 200 | 400 | 600 | 800 METRES | 1 |
| 0 | 200 | 400 | 600 YARDS | ½ | |

KILOMETRES
MILES

the huge shoulder of Ruadh-stac Mór rishing ahead, and the burn that drops in a series of waterfalls from the lip of the corrie. A final climb

beside the burn, beneath the brooding sandstone buttresses of Sàil Mhór, leads to the dramatic entrance to Coire Mhic Fhearchair.

Suddenly you emerge onto level slabs above the waterfalls **C**. Bear left and cross the burn where it flows out of the lochan, then stop to admire one of Scotland's finest mountain views. The huge crags of the Triple Buttress dominate the corrie, their gullied flanks reflected in the still waters of the little loch. The lower third is composed of red-brown Torridonian sandstone, but the upper part consists of glittering, silver-grey quartzite. In the opposite direction, the view extends over the Flowerdale Hills to the distant shores of Gairloch and Loch Ewe.

The path continues along the east side of the lochan, leading to the crags and the high ridges of Beinn Eighe, but these options are for experienced mountaineers only. Instead, take your pick of picnic sites beside the lochan, and enjoy the scenery and the remote mountain atmosphere before retracing the outward route back to Glen Torridon. ●

The stepping-stones over the Allt a' Choire Dhuibh Mhóir

The Inverianvie and Gruinard Rivers

The Inverianvie and Gruinard Rivers

Start	At the bridge that carries the A832 over the Inverianvie River 4 miles (6.5km) east of Laide
Distance	6½ miles (10.5km)
Approximate time	3½ hours
Parking	Car park opposite beach at start
Refreshments	None
Ordnance Survey maps	Landranger 19 (Gairloch & Ullapool, Loch Maree) and Pathfinders 110, NG 89/99 (Gruinard Bay) and 119, NG 88/98 (Loch Ewe)

There is wild and desolate country between these two rivers, a series of bare and craggy hills, which easily disorientate anyone new to the area. Thus a compass is essential for this walk, as is a head for heights when the narrow path climbs above the lovely Eas Dubh a' Ghlinne Ghairbh. Apart from these cautions there is nothing to detract from a walk which leads into the hills by the side of a lovely stream and, after an interlude amongst remote hills and lochs, returns on the bank of a Highland river famous for its salmon. Note that dogs must be on leads and that between September and November you should telephone 01445 731240 to make sure that there is no shooting on the hill.

From the car park, walk a few yards along the road and go through the gate immediately before you get to the bridge. Follow the river upstream. The waterfall can soon be seen ahead, and the path becomes boulder-strewn and muddy as you get closer to it. It should take about 20 minutes to reach the Eas Dubh a' Ghlinne Ghairbh **A** (aptly translated as 'the dark falls of the rough glen'), the first of a series of fine waterfalls on the Inverianvie River.

The path zigzags up a rocky staircase to reach the top of the waterfall and a narrow ravine. Here you will need both hands free as the path is narrow and there is a drop to the right. You will see primroses and violets growing in unlikely places as you climb. The scramble ends at the top of the ravine when the path reaches a broad glen with the mountains of Letterewe looming at the far end.

The path continues to follow the river to come to an enclosed area of good grass, which was once the site of a croft though now there is only a hint of the site of the building. After this the path climbs up to the top of another ravine – look back here for a

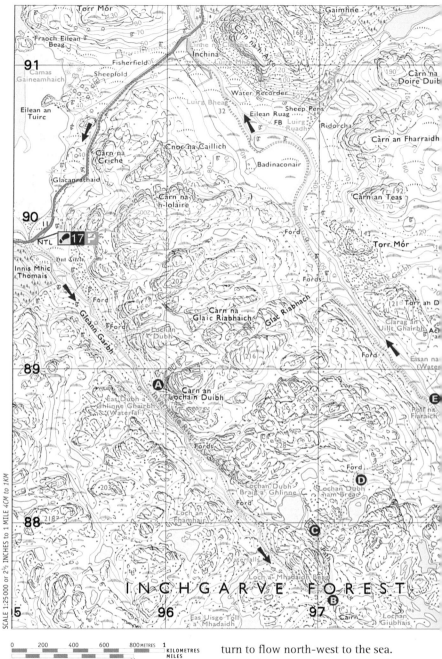

SCALE 1:25000 or 2½ INCHES to 1 MILE 4CM to 1KM

```
0    200   400   600   800 METRES  1
                                     KILOMETRES
                                     MILES
0    200   400   600 YARDS   ½
```

final view of the sea. A little further on and you are opposite another waterfall. At this point the Inverianvie, flowing from Loch a' Mhadaidh Mór, makes a right-angle turn to flow north-west to the sea. The path continues on its original course, climbing steadily and bearing left round the flank of a hill to a small cairn at a bealach (saddle) **B**.

From here the path continues bearing left, and soon you will see a loch ahead. This is Lochan Dubh

Bràig a' Ghlinne. Turn sharply to the right **C** as soon as you catch sight of the loch to leave the path and cross a small valley to the hill opposite. Now traverse north-eastwards on the lower slopes of this hill to come to another bealach, which reveals a small loch with two islands – Lochan Dubh nam Breac.

Walk to the north end of the loch **D** where a stream flows out of it and keep to the left when this divides, heading for a pointed rocky knoll. Go through the gap below the knoll, heading eastwards to the left of the whale-backed shape of Carn na Béiste, which is on the other side of the Gruinard valley. Soon after this the Gruinard River will be seen, and you can choose the easiest ground to descend the side of the valley. You will probably meet the Land Rover track near Poll na Fiaraich **E**, where the Gruinard River is joined by the Allt a' Ghlinne. The track follows the river closely for about 2 miles (3.25km) to the main road, though towards the end you can take a footpath to the left to avoid a long meander. At the main road, turn left to walk another mile (1.5km) or so to return to the starting place. ●

The Inverianvie River

Eas a' Chùal Aluinn

Start	The stalkers' path which leaves the main road (A894) to the east by the southern end of Loch na Gainmhich, 3 miles (4.75km) south of Kylesku
Distance	7 miles (11.25km)
Approximate time	4½ hours
Parking	Room for three cars at the start of the stalkers' path, otherwise park ½ mile (800m) to the north, near the loch
Refreshments	None
Ordnance Survey maps	Landranger 15 (Loch Assynt) and Pathfinder 83, NC 22/32, (Inchnadamph)

This is a far more taxing route than a quick look at the map would suggest. Although the top of the waterfall lies on about the same contour as the starting point, the walk includes demanding climbs, and some may question that the effort is worthwhile if they visit the waterfall at a time of drought. However, after a night's rain it is truly spectacular, its water dropping uninterrupted for 658ft (more than 200m), making this the highest free-falling waterfall in Britain.

From the main road at the south end of Loch na Gainmhich take the rough and boggy path that skirts the southern shore of the loch. If you look out there are sometimes otters to be seen here. The path runs along a beach but then, after crossing a stream, begins to climb steeply. The view behind becomes steadily better as you ascend with the Quinag massif dominant on the other side of the main road.

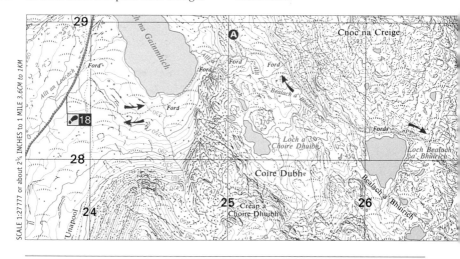

There is a brief respite from climbing as you cross a second stream, the Allt Loch Bealach a' Bhùirich. Just after this the path meets another coming up from the north end of the loch, and there is a cairn at this point **Ⓐ**. From here the path can be seen climbing to the skyline. After about an hour from the start you will reach a second cairn. Once past this you are out of sight of the road but are close to Loch Bealach a' Bhùirich.

Once the top of the bealach is reached, a wonderful view is revealed over wild country sprinkled with lochs and lochans with the Coire Gorm ridge impressive to the right. The harsh rock underfoot is gneiss, formed 2000 million years ago – ancient even in geological terms. Most of western Sutherland is composed of gneiss, as are the Outer Hebrides. The path wanders amongst barren rock, the way marked with cairns. There are good views of Eas an t-Struha Ghil, a fine waterfall on the other side of the valley.

The path fords the stream, which later becomes the waterfall **Ⓑ** – there

Eas a' Chùal Aluinn and Glen Coul

are large irregular stepping-stones and some agility is needed to make the crossing dry-shod. Beyond this the path is often over peat, which has become badly eroded in places. As it nears the waterfall it swings northwards. Eas a' Chùal Aluinn **Ⓒ** should be reached in about 2 hours from the start of the walk.

The best views of the waterfall are from a lower path to the right, where the tumbling water makes an exciting foreground to views of Loch Beag. Walk about 150 yds (137m) along the edge of the Leitir Dhubh ('dark cliffs') to find this path. You will often see deer from this vantage-point.

The Gaelic form of the waterfall's name means 'the splendid falls of Glen Coul' though many will feel that 19th-century English visitors bestowed more romance on it when they called it 'The Maiden's Tresses'. Eas a' Chùal Aluinn lies on the fault-line that runs south-eastwards down Glen Coul and at 658ft (200m) it is three times higher than Niagara.

The same route is used for the return but if you have parked at the north end of the loch it is advisable to follow the outward route to the road to have an easy walk back to your parking-place.　●

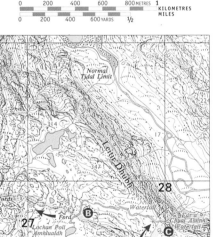

Glen Brittle and Glen Eynort

Start	Eynort village by the bridge over the Eynort River, Skye
Distance	10½ miles (16.75km)
Approximate time	4½ hours
Parking	Near bridge at start
Refreshments	None
Ordnance Survey maps	Landranger 32 (South Skye), Outdoor Leisure 8 (The Cuillin & Torridon Hills) and Pathfinder 202 NG 32 (Loch Eynort)

This is an invigorating but fairly level forest walk, which gives a succession of panoramas of the two glens. The fairyland shapes of the Cuillins dominate Glen Brittle, while the hills overlooking Loch Eynort are less dramatic and the views are given scale by the cottages and pastures of the glen. This is an ideal walk for a 'soft' (i.e. damp) Skye day or on one when a gale is blowing.

Drive down Glen Eynort until, just before the telephone-box, a road goes off to the left. This crosses a bridge and then a cattle-grid. Park off the road before the latter.

Glen Brittle and the Cuillins, Skye

Walk across the cattle-grid and then turn left off the road up a forestry track, past a green gate. The way climbs steeply round a hairpin bend. Pass a waterfall on the left – to the right there are views over Loch Eynort. Another hairpin bend takes

The falls at Grula

you over the stream again, and once more there is another waterfall to admire. Look back from here for a different aspect of the loch. The track climbs round a third hairpin bend and, 300 yds (274m) after this, turn left **A** on to a level track through the forest. Even though the walking is easy and the views restricted by trees there is still much to see. Goldcrests and goldfinches are small birds to look out for here, while birds of prey range from the kestrel and the peregrine falcon to the majesty of the eagle. Golden eagles are sometimes seen soaring above Glen Brittle, while sea eagles favour the Loch Eynort side of the hill.

After a little way, a clearing gives views of the twin knolls that make up Cnoc Scarall and the steep road leading through Glen Eynort. After this, views are screened by the forest for a time before the road reaches a point where the Cuillins can be seen. Streams flowing from Beinn a' Bhràghad down deeply etched gullies allow views of this summit to the right. All this time the track has been climbing steadily. At the crest of the hill there is a clearing and then a quarry. Just after the quarry take the track to the right **B**.

This track heads south-eastwards parallel to the Glen Brittle road. It gives views of the Cuillins, which are constantly changing as you progress, and comes close to the road opposite

a picnic site **C** (an alternative starting point). Look across the glen from here and you will see the ravines that hide the delightful Fairy Pools (see Walk 13). Both road and track swing south-westwards from here, the latter keeping to higher ground. The track then passes through an area of harvested timber, and this clearance gives even more extensive views over Glen Brittle and down to the loch. To the right there is a different view of Beinn a' Bhràghad to that seen earlier.

After this, the prospect is screened by trees, and the track climbs steadily. When it emerges again there is an impressive view of Loch Brittle, with An Cruachan the flat-topped hill ahead. This is the start of Bealach Brittle, an enjoyable short ascent with a good spot at the top **D** to pause for a picnic and take in the grand view of the Cuillins in their incomparable setting. After the summit of the pass the track enters forest again. Keep ahead when a track joins from the left, coming from the lochside at Kraiknish. Before the planting of the forestry this was known as the Cuckoo Path. It must have been an enchanting way down to Loch Eynort when there were fewer trees to hide its shores. Keep ahead again when another track leaves to the right **E**. Shortly after this junction Loch Eynort suddenly comes into view, and the harvesting of trees allows extensive views. The track leads through the handful of houses at Grula to become a metalled road. There is a spectacular waterfall on the right here. The starting point is less than ½ mile (800m) along the road from this point. ●

The Beinn na Caillich Horseshoe

The Beinn na Caillich Horseshoe

Start	At the end of the short lane signposted to 'Old Corry' off the A87, 1 mile (1.5km) north-west of Broadford, Skye
Distance	5 miles (8km)
Approximate time	5 hours
Parking	Spaces off the road near the start (do not park in the turning area)
Refreshments	None
Ordnance Survey maps	Landranger 32 (South Skye) and Outdoor Leisure 8 (The Cuillin & Torridon Hills)

This is a surprisingly hard excursion, mainly due to the steep climb up to Beinn na Caillich ('the mountain of the old woman'), which is only a Corbett of 2400ft (732m) but feels much more because of the large boulders that hinder the ascent. However, the ridge walk is exhilarating and gives comprehensive views over southern Skye and the Knoydart and Applecross peninsulas. The descent down 750ft (229m) of scree from the summit of Beinn Dearg Mhór is also exciting, though people nervous of unstable surfaces will not appreciate this section. The route should not be attempted unless you are sure of good conditions.

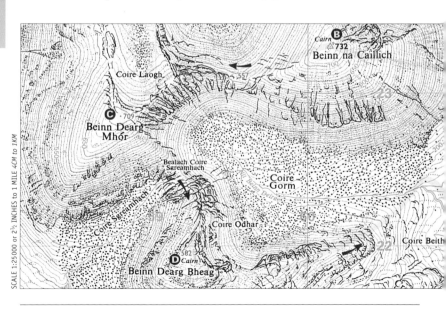

SCALE 1:25000 or 2½ INCHES to 1 MILE 4CM to 1KM

The house at the end of the lane is called Coire-chat-achan ('Corrie of the Cats') and is a successor of the Mackinnon homestead where Johnson and Boswell were guests in 1773. The Mackinnons were tenants of Sir Alexander Macdonald of Armadale, and the two travellers seem to have enjoyed their stay even though the small house was constantly thronged with locals hoping to meet the distinguished visitors. Only a fragment of wall survives of this house.

From the end of the lane continue ahead to a burn, cross it and then turn right. Turn right again when you reach a wall, which will lead you to another stream **A**. Keep this to the right as you climb the lower slopes of Beinn na Caillich until the stream suddenly bends to the right. Already there are fine views of Broadford and across the water to Ben Nevis and the Moidart mountains.

As you approach the boulders that form a giant's staircase up the hill,

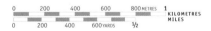

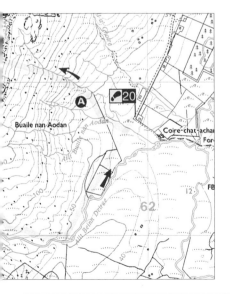

you are faced with the choice whether to risk your ankles in striding from one granite boulder to another or to stick to the steep heather slope for as long as possible. Both ways sap stamina, and eventually you will be forced to struggle through or over the boulders. It is a comfort to know that the gradient eases towards the top, where the way is close to the edge of the spectacular Coire Fearchair.

If you reach the summit cairn **B** in less than 2 hours you will have done well. It must be amongst the largest of all cairns, having a circumference of nearly 150ft (46m). It is supposed to be the burial place of a Viking princess, and though Norway may not be in view here most of Skye and much of western Scotland can be seen. From this point the ridge that takes the route westwards to Beinn Dearg Mhór looks razor-sharp and leads the eye onwards to the western group of Red Hills, so named because they are made of a pink granite which breaks down into a gritty scree that is almost impossible to climb. Beyond the Red Hills the jagged peaks of the Cuillins can be seen.

The narrow ridge takes you above Coire Gorm to the south and Coire Reidh to the north and gives you the feeling of walking in the sky. The ridge descends to a bealach (Coire Laogh) before a short climb brings you to the summit of Beinn Dearg Mhór, which also has a substantial cairn **C** set on a wide boulder-strewn plateau. The next part of the route is the most demanding, and care needs to be taken both in navigation and execution. From the summit turn left to descend south-eastwards to the Bealach Coire Sgreamhach. The scree slope is of small coarse-grained fragments of red granite, which should not present problems in good conditions unless taken too quickly. A consolation to the damage being done to boots is that the slope would be almost impossible to climb. Try to pause occasionally to take in the wonderful views over Loch Slapin to the right.

It is almost frightening to look back up the 750-ft (229m) high scree slope from the bealach. However, the next climb is to the summit of Beinn Dearg Bheag Ⓓ, which is an easy ascent over boulders and rock. This third peak offers more stunning views, especially to the south to the islands of Rum, Eigg and Canna. A feature of this walk is that you are seldom out of sight of human habitation, a kind of reassurance in such wild surroundings. The marble works on Loch Slapin are distinctive, sending out milkiness into the loch.

Coire Gorm from Beinn na Caillich

Continue to follow the ridge, now heading eastwards as it descends above the vast bowl of Coire Gorm. There are more magnificent views, even at this late stage. Towards the bottom, the going degenerates into sheep-tracks threading through boulders and heather. Keep on the ridge for as long as possible before beginning to bear left over extremely rough and moist ground to reach the Allt Beinn Deirge, the burn flowing from the corrie. Every time this descent is made one has the conviction that there must be an easier way off the hill. However, there is a consensus that the left (northern) bank of the stream should be followed. As you come to a sheep enclosure, which heralds the end of the walk, note the way in which the stream has etched a cliff into the glacial deposit through which it flows. From here it is but a short step back to the starting point. ●

Sandwood Bay

Start	Blairmore, about 2½ miles (4km) north-west of Kinlochbervie, where the track to Sandwood Bay leaves to the right
Distance	9 miles (14.5km)
Approximate time	4½ hours
Parking	Limited off-road parking at start
Refreshments	None
Ordnance Survey maps	Landranger 9 (Cape Wrath) and Pathfinders 43 NC 16/26 (Strath Shinary) and 52, NC 15 (Ardmore Point)

The fame of Sandwood Bay's beauty has spread, so the walk there by way of the moorland track is now a popular trek for tourists in the area. This route uses the track for the return but makes a delightful approach to the beauty-spot over heather-covered hills and clifftops. Note that the path ends less than 2 miles (3.25km) from Sheigra, and after this the going is rough. However, it would be hard to become lost with the sea so close, and the reward is a wonderful approach to a remote and romantic place. You may well meet seals on the beach, the ghost of an old sailor in seaboots, or even mermaids, which were frequently sighted here in days gone by.

Walk along the made-up road towards Sheigra. Within a few yards you come into Balchrick, like Blairmore a place comprised of six or so homesteads. There are lovely views to the left over the coastline and to the mountains of Assynt. Pass the post office and bear right when the road forks. The road ends but the track continues ahead at Sheigra **A**. At first it climbs through enclosed sheep pastures but soon reaches a gate leading on to open moorland.

About half an hour's walking brings you to a point from where you can see Loch na Gainimh to the right with a fine array of mountains beyond and the track used for the return on its far side. The track is still climbing gently when it suddenly swings left and you get a sight of the sea ahead. Unfortunately, it deteriorates from here into a rocky path and then ends quite abruptly **B**, seeming to lead you quite deliberately into a peat-bog. The track was originally made to reach the peat-diggings here.

Continue to head towards the sea but bear slightly right to cross the Allt Lochan a' Phuirt Bhig and climb to the ridge on its eastern side. Then make for the sea again, with Am Baig, the island about 1 mile (1.5km) offshore, to the left. You should now be about ½ mile (800m) east of Port

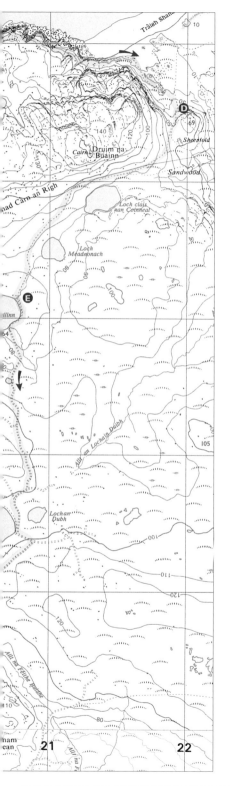

Beag, with the next objective being the crossing of the Allt Lochan a' Mhuillinn (and the fence that follows its valley) to climb Carn an Righ. From this summit **C** there is a good view of the rocky beach at Port Mòr and, to the right, you can just see the tip of Am Buachaille 'The Shepherd', a needle-like rock stack 200ft (61m) high, which must pose a powerful challenge to any cliff cragsman; it was first climbed in 1967. Climb a little further and not only do you see the rest of Am Buachaille in its little bay but also the whole length of coastline. which culminates in Cape Wrath, the north-western tip of Scotland. The cliffs are formidable and reach a climax to the east of the Cape in Cléit Dhubh, a precipitous cliff that at 850ft (259m) is the highest in Britain.

As you continue round the headland (Rubh a' Buachaille) you can see the regular jointing of the rock in the cliff-face, which illustrates how easily such structures are formed by the constant erosion of the sea. Take care as you skirt the clifftop, and look for places where the soil has dropped, betraying the underlying weaknesses, which will soon result in another portion of cliff slipping beneath the waves.

Continue along the cliffs a little further and Sandwood Bay comes into view, together with its loch which lies behind the sand dunes. The view is truly magnificent with the sparkling white beach, often unblemished by human footprint, serving as a foreground to the cliff-girt shoreline which, if visibility allows, ends with the speck of the lighthouse at the tip of Cape Wrath.

0	200	400	600	800 METRES	1	
						KILOMETRES
						MILES
0	200	400	600 YARDS		1/2	

Follow a distinct path along the edge of the cliffs to descend to the beach down beneath the crags of Druim na Buainn, which overlooks the southern end of the bay. If you are lucky enough to visit Sandwood on a good day you will not want to hurry away from the place. Seals often lie on the sand near the tideline, and it is easy to trip over one – to mutual shock – if a wind is blowing to camouflage them with drifting sand. The dunes show the tracks of the many birds and animals, and you may well see the spoor of a wildcat, the impressions of its claws in the sand making it unmistakable.

Leave the beach by climbing over the dunes at its south-western end. The path begins **D** over the wide grassy sward near a sheepfold. Pass about 100 yds (91m) above this to head south west. The long-deserted Sandwood House can be seen below to the left. This was the haunt of a bearded and sea-booted sailor, one of several ghosts reported from Sandwood in the last fifty years or so. None of them leave footprints as they walk across the dunes.

Sandwood Bay

The path climbs steadily below the southern slopes of Druim na Buainn. There is a fence to the right and Loch Clais nan Coinneal is to the left as the top of the pass is reached. The track is being eroded by walkers seeking dry ways across the peat hags, which widens it without improving the going. The land now belongs to the John Muir Trust, and it is probably their volunteers who have improved things by piling loose stones into cairns. The course of the path can be seen for miles ahead, winding over the moorland.

It skirts a smaller loch before coming to lovely Loch a' Mhuillinn **E** where it follows the sandy beach on the eastern side. The loch brings relief to the bleak landscape, and the scene is also given interest by the distant sight of the Assynt mountains. After passing a lochan the surface of the path improves. It is used by motorists as far as Loch na Gainimh, and many people park by its shore to shorten the distance to Sandwood. From here it is 2 miles (3.25km) to Blairmore, and the walking is easy, with a fine view facing you as you come to the end of the circuit. ●

A Circuit of Beinn Alligin

Start	The car park by the bridge above Torridon House, 2 miles (3.25km) west of Torridon village
Distance	8 miles (12.75km)
Approximate time	5½ hours
Parking	At start
Refreshments	Pubs and tearoom in Torridon village
Ordnance Survey maps	Landranger 24 (Raasay, Applecross & Loch Torridon) and Outdoor Leisure 8 (The Cuillin & Torridon Hills)

The usual way to climb Beinn Alligin is by following the path by the stream that runs down Coire Mhic Nòbuil. However, this route is a walk rather than a climb, and though an easy way is suggested to the summit en route, this is optional, and the excursion is primarily a way of exploring remote country by climbing through the Bealach a' Chòmhla and traversing rough ground on the flanks of one of Torridon's grandest mountains. Attempt this route only in good visibility.

The path from the bridge initially follows the stream through trees and rhododendrons but soon emerges on to the hillside, and Beinn Alligin comes into view on the left. The mountain is divided into two: on the left is the principal summit of Sgurr Mhór (3231ft/986m), which is distinctive for being cleft with the Eag Dhuibh, a savage gash that splits the southern face in half; to the right are the famous Horns of Alligin, the three peaks that give the mountain a prehistoric look – a fancy that is appropriate since its Torridonian sandstone is more than 1000 million years old and is amongst the most ancient sedimentary rocks, laid down at a time when there was no oxygen and thus no life on our planet.

The walking at this stage is easy and enjoyable on a well-used path. The first bridge over the burn –

½ mile (800m) from the road bridge and close to the waterfalls – was dismantled in 1994 because the path onward was becoming badly eroded. About 30 minutes' walking brings you to the bridge over the Abhainn Coire Mhic Nòbuil **Ⓐ**. After this the path follows a lesser stream. Keep

The view north from Carn Doineig

SCALE 1:25000 or 2½ INCHES to 1 MILE 4CM to 1KM

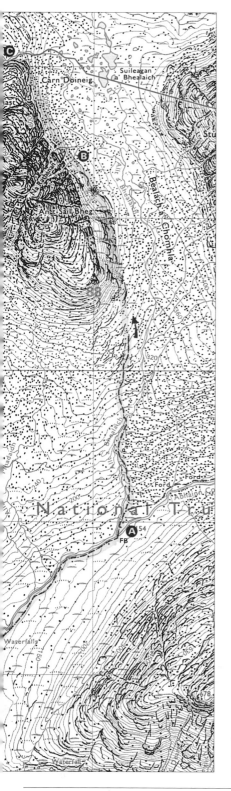

ahead after the bridge when the path divides at a cairn. The path to the right leads to Coire Dubh Mór below Beinn Eighe and then to the Kinlochewe road. Cross a bridge over the burn (Allt a' Bhealaich). To the left, Beinn Alligin's grandest corrie dominates the scene – this is Coire Toll a' Mhadaidh, the lair of the last wolf to be killed in the district, early in the 18th century. After the bridge the going becomes steeper and more rocky, but to compensate, the view back to Loch Torridon improves all the time. Liathach is well seen to the east. Keep the stream to the right as the path ceases to climb and becomes less distinct.

A good place to pause is where a tumbling burn flowing from the crags to the left is crossed **B**. It would be hard to find water more refreshing than this. Two hours from the start the path, by now extremely vague, reaches a place where you can overlook the lochans at the crest of the bealach (Sùileagan a' Bhealaich). Soon after this a waterfall will be seen to the left **C**. It is fed by the waters of Loch Toll nam Biast. Climb up by the waterfall and then follow the stream to reach two small lochans and then the larger loch. Keep a sharp lookout for golden eagles scouting over this lonely countryside.

Follow the southern shore of Loch Toll nam Biast. The terrain is extremely rocky and can be wet. As you begin to turn south-westwards round the flank of the mountain **D**, a grassy slope will be seen leading up to Sgurr Mhór, the principal summit of Beinn Alligin. You may well be tempted to make the relatively easy ascent from this point if you have not

0	200	400	600	800 METRES	1	
						KILOMETRES
						MILES
0	200	400	600 YARDS	½		

climbed the mountain before. The tiny shapes of walkers on the ridge above confirm that they are about 1000ft (300m) above you here.

The route continues to skirt the Ben giving ever-improving views out to sea towards Lewis, Harris and the Shiant Islands. It is difficult to avoid the innumerable small burns which flow from Beinn Alligin's western corries (An Réidh-choire). However, by now you have turned to the south and are beginning to descend. A cottage with a distinctive red roof on the far side of Loch Torridon makes a good landmark to aim at, and a deer fence will come into sight below as the view becomes even more spectacular, taking in Loch Torridon, Skye and the Applecross peninsula. Go through the fence at a convenient place **E** shortly before it makes a right-angle bend and descends. Keep the fence to the left as you descend the rough and often moist ground to the road. Once on solid ground, follow the road eastwards back to the starting point.

Beinn Alligin

Rubh' an Dùnain from Glen Brittle

Start	Glen Brittle campsite, Skye
Distance	8½ miles (13.5km)
Approximate time	5 hours
Parking	Car park at end of public road in Glen Brittle
Refreshments	None
Ordnance Survey maps	Landranger 32 (South Skye) and Outdoor Leisure 8 (The Cuillin & Torridon Hills)

This coastal walk demands more energy than it might seem at first sight. Rubh' an Dùnain could be called the Scottish Tintagel and has the same aura of mystery and romance. A reasonably good coastal path leads directly to the headland with its ancient fort and settlement but a more circuitous approach is suggested here, which allows even finer views of a magnificent coastline.

Follow the road straight through the campsite to a path behind the white-painted toilet block. Cross the stile and then bear right away from the main path, which leads to the west-facing corries at the heart of the Cuillins. Our path passes water tanks and then follows the eastern shore of Loch Brittle along the edge of cliffs. Canna is the closest of the offshore islands at this point. At first there is rock underfoot but this gives way to springy turf after a burn is crossed.

You will meet a more substantial stream about 1 mile (1.5km) from the start – the Allt Coire Làgan – and if this is in spate you may have to divert upstream to cross it by a bridge **A** just below the Land Rover track which runs parallel to the coastal path higher up the slope. There are lovely waterfalls here which provide foregrounds for spectacular views of the Cuillins.

Two more small burns are crossed but there is a considerable distance before the next one as cliffs to the left get steeper and draw nearer. Turn left off the main path at this latter stream **B** on to a lesser path that climbs with it up the hill to reach a beautiful lochan which photographers will recognise as providing another good foreground for views of the mountains. From here the next objective is the ascent of Creag Mhór; make for the further of the two summits.

This provides a wonderful panorama of Hebridean islands. Canna, Rum and Eigg lie close at hand to the south while South Uist and Barra can be seen to the west.

From Creag Mhór descend to the wall which cuts off the extremity of the peninsula. This is an ancient boundary known as Slochd Dubh (the Black Drain). Go through the wall **C**

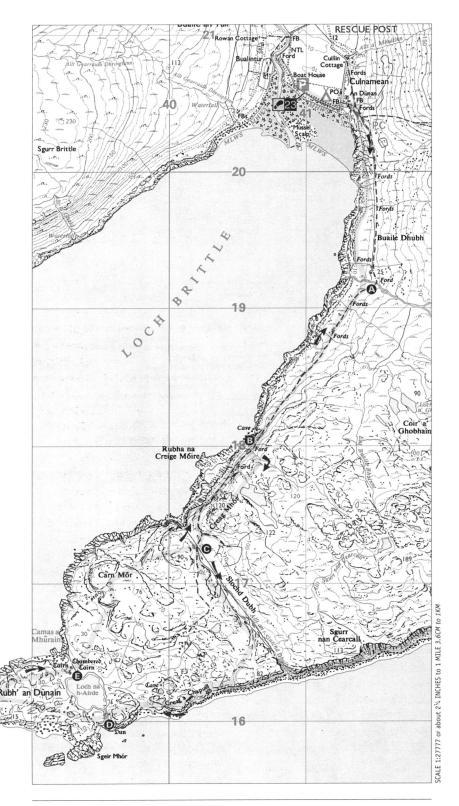

SCALE 1:27777 or about 2¼ INCHES to 1 MILE 3.6CM to 1KM

The Cuillins from Creag Mhór

and turn left to follow it south-eastwards. The wall has become fairly ruinous so it is easy to cross from one side to the other to avoid boggy areas. After about ¼ mile (400m) the path to Rubh' an Dùnain branches off to the right. Continue to follow the wall until the sea comes into view ahead and the wall reaches the deep cleft made by Allt an Slochd Dubh. Bear right and walk across the heather to the edge of the cliffs and then turn westwards to follow them to Rubh' an Dùnain. Soay, famous for its breed of sheep, is the island just offshore. Loch na h-Airde will soon be seen below with the ruined croft of Rhundunan, once the home of the MacAskill clan.

To reach the headland you have to cross the Boat Channel **D**, the outlet made from the loch by the MacAskills. Originally it was navigable but it has since been blocked by boulders, which makes it easy to cross. The Dun (an Iron Age fort) stands on the eastern side of the channel. One of its walls has

miraculously managed to survive the onslaught of the elements over four thousand or so years.

The return from Rubh' an Dùnain begins by skirting the shore of Loch na h-Airde to the wall midway along its northern side. Go through the gap; a well-preserved neolithic chambered cairn is a few yards to the right here **E**. From the gap, take the left-hand path leading towards Loch Brittle, heading a little to the left of the Cuillins. Rich grassland conceals any trace of a path, but now head for the topmost Cuillin pinnacle, Sgurr Dearg, to reach a rocky stairway leading up to Carn Mór. Keep heading eastward over this top and you will descend to the Slochd Dubh wall **C**.

The way now skirts the seaward slopes of Creag Mhór. At first it is boggy, and you may find it easier to follow a turf bank, which leads towards drier ground. However, by heading towards Loch Brittle you will soon find a discernible path, which brings the campsite into view though it is about 2½ miles (4km) distant. The scenery is fine compensation for weariness, and you will also be able to watch seals and seabirds fishing the waters below as you retrace your way back to the start. ●

| 0 | 200 | 400 | 600 | 800 METRES | 1 |
| 0 | 200 | 400 | 600 YARDS | ½ |

KILOMETRES
MILES

Loch an Draing and Camas Mór from Cove

Loch an Draing and Camas Mór from Cove

Start	Cove, at the end of the road (B8057) running up the eastern shore of Loch Ewe from Poolewe
Distance	10 miles (16km)
Approximate time	6 hours
Parking	At the end of the B8057
Refreshments	None
Ordnance Survey maps	Landranger 19 (Gairloch & Ullapool, Loch Maree) and Pathfinders 109, NG 79/89 (Melvaig & Rubha Réidh) and 110, NG 89/99 (Gruinard Bay)

This walk is exhilarating but should not be undertaken lightly. The going is invariably rough and often extremely wet. The distance of 10 miles (16km) is a rough calculation since for much of the way there is no path. It could be longer or shorter, depending on how closely you follow the coastline and the detours you make to avoid wet ground. The coastal scenery is magnificent, while Loch an Draing is a place of true magic.

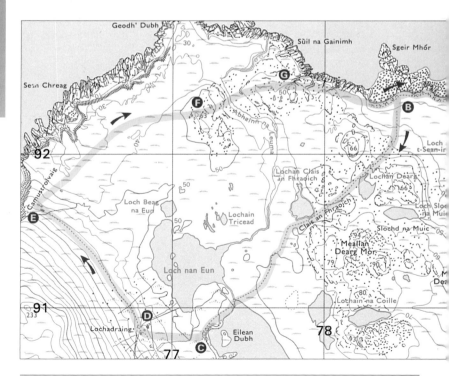

The road ends at the old gun emplacements on Rubha nan Sàsan, built to defend Loch Ewe, which was important as a marshalling-point for convoys during the Second World War. Walk past these to the end of the track and cross a rocky beach to skirt the seaward side of the crag on the opposite side. There is a fairly obvious path to follow at first, which only disappears when it crosses exposed rock. Improvised stepping-stones have been made over some particularly boggy parts.

After about 30 minutes you round a headland, following the path along a rocky ledge, and radio masts come into sight ahead. The larger island offshore is Eilean Furadh Mór, which saw a tragic shipwreck on 26 February 1944 when the American Liberty ship USS *William H. Welsh* went ashore here in terrible

conditions. Despite heroic efforts by crofters, who struggled through a blizzard to reach this remote shore, there were only twelve survivors from a crew of seventy-four. The remains of one of the stricken ship's lifeboats can be seen on the shore opposite the island **Ⓐ**; there is another rusty hulk at the north end of the next bay.

From here the path becomes even more vague and wet. The headland (Stac Ruadh) has a cairn, and the path passes to the left of this. The wonderful view takes in the islands of Lewis and Harris as well as Skye. Soon the low headland of Sgeir Mhór comes into view on the far side of a rocky strand with one small patch of sand suitable for cooling your feet if the tide is favourable. Below the radio masts a track can be seen climbing up the Clais an Fhraoich. Walk along the top of a storm beach (large boulders thrown up haphazardly by the force of the waves) and, almost at the end,

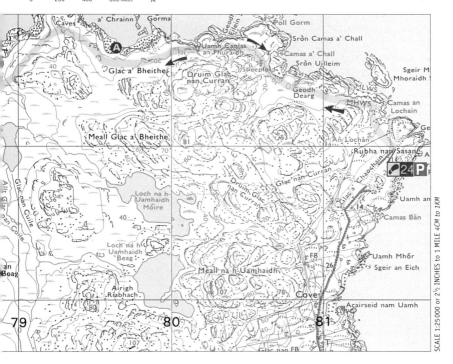

turn left to the end of the rocky track noted above **B**. It will have taken you nearly 90 minutes of hard walking to reach this point.

The track climbs steadily to reach Lochan Dearg, and then there is level ground before it passes another lochan, this one to the right. A very boggy section follows before the path climbs round a shoulder of the hill and Loch an Draing is suddenly revealed below with its lesser neighbour, Loch nan Eun. These lochs occupy the channel formed by the Loch Maree fault, which bisects this peninsula following a south-easterly direction. The two lochs are joined by a stream, which is crossed by a bridge. Go through the gate and follow the path round the northern end of the loch, enjoying wonderful views of Beinn Eighe and Slioch. There is an enchanting birch grove by the loch as you crest a rise and see the deserted croft of Lochadraing on the other side of the valley. On a hot day the mossy ground beneath the birches makes a wonderful place for a picnic or a rest.

Shortly you will come to another extremely boggy section of path. It is best to swing to the right off the path before this **C** and head up towards Lochadraing, where a steel gate gives a way through the sheep-fence. From the old croft **D** a track goes seawards along the flank of the hill. There are more outstanding views from this track, which eventually reaches Camustrolvaig, another abandoned croft, where part of one building has been restored as a shepherd's shelter. A few yards further on, you come to the edge of the cliff **E** above Camas Mór, a wonderful beach of silver sand which is reached by a steep zigzag path that looks fearsome but is actually easily descended.

The way back sounds straightforward but demands considerable effort. Put simply, you follow the coast back to the start. However, at the edge of the cliffs there are steep synclines to negotiate, while further inland ancient peat workings make progress equally laborious. It is probably best to make for the hill to the north of Loch nan Eun **F**, which wears a cairn on its summit. It is an excellent viewpoint, especially for the onward route. Look seawards towards Eilean Furadh Mór. Just to the right of the island you can see a hill that seems to have two cairns **G**. In fact, there is only one cairn, the other proves to be an enormous free-standing boulder. From this hill you can see the storm beach **B** where you joined the path to Loch an Draing earlier. From here follow the coastal path back to the start; it could well take you more than the 90 minutes it took on the outward route. ●

Loch an Draing

Lower Diabaig and Leacan Bàna from Inveralligin

Start	Inveralligin on the north shore of Loch Torridon
Distance	8½ miles (13.5km)
Approximate time	5½ hours
Parking	Roadside parking near the start
Refreshments	None
Ordnance Survey maps	Landranger 24 (Raasay, Applecross & Loch Torridon), Pathfinder 155, NG 65/75 (Arinacrinachd) and Outdoor Leisure 8 (The Cuillin & Torridon Hills)

Many of the best walks in the North-West Highlands follow coastline paths. The path snaking over Leacan Bàna, the rugged cliffs at the western end of the north shore of Loch Torridon, gives views of sea and mountain that can hardly be rivalled, even in this area. Later, the path strikes inland across rough moorland to reach Lower Diabaig, a village in an idyllic setting, looking out to the Western Isles. The return entails climbing steeply at first on a path that eventually takes you to the road by Loch a' Mhullaich. There are two occasions where you may leave the road to take 'short cuts' on the old road over the hill, but by this time most people will prefer the easy walking on smooth tarmac. Note that the path involves some gentle scrambling and that some of the drops to the sea are long and vertical.

The walk begins from the telephone-box at Inveralligin. Take the track, which branches off the road to the right at this point, and cross the bridge. Pass in front of cottages on to a path above the beach. Immediately before the Field Centre, turn right to follow a zigzag path that climbs to moorland. There are fine views of Loch Torridon and Beinn All-gin.

The path wanders across the moor to join the lane through Alligin Shuas. Keep ahead on the road, but after ½ mile (800m) bear left **A** down the hill. When the surfaced road ends, the track continues for a few yards to a white cottage. The path goes to the right here, following the fence at first and then climbing through bracken into a coppiced birch wood. Cross a burn and go through a metal gate on to a path that climbs the flank of a hill. As height is gained the views improve, with lochside cottages and traffic on the main road vital in giving scale to the panorama. There is a tricky section where the path climbs steeply on exposed earth with a steep drop to the left. The views eastwards up the

SCALE 1:27 777 or about 2¼ INCHES to 1 MILE 3.6CM to 1KM

```
0      200    400    600    800 METRES 1
                                        KILOMETRES
                                        MILES
0      200    400    600 YARDS  ½
```

loch to Liathach are superb and Beinn Damh is prominent on the south side of Loch Torridon.

Bear right when the path divides **B**. After this the going becomes more difficult, and there are rocky staircases as the path gradually swings westwards and passes behind a white cottage, an exceptionally remote home, which relies on a boat for transport. Beyond the cottage is

Lochan Dubh, soon followed by Loch a' Bhealaich Mhóir, the latter particularly lovely when its water-lilies are in bloom.

After this you climb through a rocky valley, and at the top Lower Diabaig comes into view with the Outer Hebridean islands of Harris and Lewis in the distance. The path skirts the hill high above the quay, and at this point care is needed in negotiating loose stone. After an old gate it descends through tall bracken to reach the shore by a white house.

Loch Torridon from Leacan Bàna

burn to the left and a wire fence to the right.

Keep climbing steadily to reach the crest of the Bealach na Gaoithe – the Pass of the Winds. Go through a gate here and then along the top end of Loch a' Mhullaich to reach the road **D**. Turn right. After almost a mile (1.5km) there is a gate by the ruins of a croft above Loch Diabaigas Airde.

*You can, if you prefer, leave the road at this point **E** and cross the fields to the top end of the loch (you will have to inch your way round the fence that projects into the water). The path then climbs steadily to reach the road at the top of Bealach na Gaoithe. There is certainly satisfaction in following this ancient way, which crofters would have used for centuries before the building of the modern road.*

After 600 yds (549m) a further length of footpath cuts off a corner after a lochan where the road swings right to descend in a wide zigzag **F**. This is certainly better than following the road. From here the walking is downhill on the road and 1½ miles (2.5km) back is soon covered. ●

The gate here carries a notice (for those walking in the other direction) warning that the path is precipitous.

Unfortunately, Diabaig has nothing to offer in the way of refreshment though it is a place of great peace and beauty. The walk continues by retracing your steps up the path by the house to a byre **C** and then following close to the Allt an Uain, passing another byre, this one with a corrugated iron roof. The going is steep and the path vague at times but it is hard to go wrong thanks to the

Camasunary, Elgol and Glasnakille

Start	South-west of Kirkibost, Skye, where a track on the right leaves the B8083 (opposite a layby)
Distance	9½ miles (15.25km)
Approximate time	6 hours
Parking	Layby about ½ mile (800m) beyond a turn to the left off B8083 to Kilmarie Old Church
Refreshments	None
Ordnance Survey maps	Landranger 32 (South Skye) and Outdoor Leisure 8 (The Cuillin & Torridon Hills)

This is a long but not over-strenuous walk taking you to a remote beauty spot (Camasunary) that gives a hint of the spectacular splendour of the Cuillins. From here a cliff path follows the coastline to Elgol (be warned that there are a few places where the path is narrow above a long drop to the sea). From Elgol the way crosses to the east coast of the peninsula and returns by quiet roads and unfrequented paths, which give wonderful views over Lochs Slapin and Eishort. You may like to include swimming-gear in your haversack.

At the start the inviting track can be seen winding across moorland towards the mountains past clumps of conifers. Walk up this track, which after about 20 minutes reaches a gate. After this it passes a cairn and becomes much rougher. Suddenly Loch Scavaig is revealed far below with the fantastic pinnacles of the Cuillins beyond and the white house (Camasunary) perfectly situated on the strand below helping to give scale to the scene.

You catch a glimpse of remote Loch na Crèitheach before the path begins its steep zigzag descent to the shore. The islands seen far out on the horizon are South Uist and Barra – Soay, Eigg Rum and Canna are closer

at hand. Turn sharply to the left **A** at a junction of paths just before a little bridge. Continuing on the other path would take you to Loch na Crèitheach and Glen Sligachan.

The path leads down to a grassy shoreline. Turn left (if you can ignore the appeal of the lovely beach) and when the shore ends at a rocky outcrop climb to find a faint path that runs southwards along the low cliffs. This part of the route is rough and wet, and the path often runs above vertical drops as it twists through clumps of birches. However, the scenery is a compensation, and eventually the path descends steeply to reach a rock-strewn beach where Glen Scaladal meets the sea **B**. Cross

Camasunary, Skye

the streams and look across Loch Scavaig to see a magnificent waterfall tumbling into the sea from Gars-bheinn.

Climb up the steep hill on the south side of the beach to the clifftop path, which now runs beneath the crags of Ben Cleat – there are further tricky sections here. However, the coastal scenery, both forward and back, is even more spectacular from here. When Elgol ('Holy Hill') comes into view ahead you will need to head up the grassy slopes to a gate in the fence just above the nearest cottage. Go through this and walk down the track to reach the main road and the village. Turn left and climb the hill.

A few yards before the post office (a corrugated iron shed) turn right off the road **C** to follow a line of posts that head directly for a road, which

can be seen climbing a hill on the other side of the small valley. Cross the stream and go through an iron gate on the other side. A second stream is crossed by a delightful little stone bridge, which would be called a clapper bridge on Dartmoor. Keep ahead to the road and turn left to follow its tortuous course past radio masts. At a T-junction by a telephone-box in Glasnakille, turn left. This short length of road gives fine views over Loch Slapin and ends at a croft **D**.

From here the way continues as a beautiful birch-fringed track descending to cross a stream. It then emerges from woodland to pass a new house, and beyond this there is a surfaced road. The road climbs steadily but, when there is a brief respite from the ascent and it makes a sweeping left-hand turn, take the track which goes ahead **E** towards a white cottage.

About 50 yds (46m) before the cottage take a faint track to the right **F**, which descends and follows the shoreline of the loch. This passes the site of a long-abandoned croft to reach a gate in the deer-fence sited close to an ancient fort. There is a stone seat on the left just before a new bungalow. After this follow the drive to the road. This leads past an old graveyard and the big house of Kilmarie. The village was an early centre of Christianity in Skye and gets its name from St Maolrubha, an obscure missionary saint who established a church here. The road then follows the lovely river and passes disused kennels to the main road. Turn left to walk back to the starting point. ●

0	200	400	600	800 METRES	1	
						KILOMETRES
						MILES
0	200	400	600 YARDS	½		

Raasay – Dùn Caan and the Burma Road

Start	Ferry pier, Raasay
Distance	10 miles (16km)
Approximate time	6 hours
Parking	Car park at Sconser, Skye
Refreshments	Isle of Raasay Hotel and Outdoor Centre
Ordnance Survey maps	Landranger 24 (Raasay, Applecross & Loch Torridon) and Pathfinders 187, NG 43/53 (Narrows of Raasay) and 171, NG 44/54 (Portree)

The lovely island of Raasay lies between Skye and the Applecross peninsula and is reached by a ferry sailing from Sconser. The island was privately owned for many years and has only recently been made accessible to tourists. This walk takes into account the ferry timetable – a day visitor will most likely take the 9.30 a.m. sailing, which gives nearly 8 hours on the island, plenty of time to complete this delightful round, which includes a visit to the summit of Dùn Caan, a superb viewpoint for Raasay, Skye and much of the coastline of the western Highlands.

From the Ferry Pier on Raasay, turn left along the road. The steep, straight incline facing you as you leave the ferry was built during World War I as part of extensive iron-ore workings. The incline is the final part of the return leg of this walk. The road hugs the shore and leads past the war memorial to enter Inverarish village.

Turn left after the telephone boxes **A** and pass the church at the top of the hill. The Isle of Raasay Hotel is to the right and, shortly after this, the Raasay Outdoor Centre to the left, now occupying Raasay House. This is where Johnson and Boswell stayed when they were on Raasay in 1773.

The ruins of Saint Molnag's Chapel are seen to the right. The road passes through a short stretch or forest and when it emerges from the trees there is a fine view onwards over Oskaig. Camastianavaig is the small village on the other side of the Narrows of Raasay, sheltering beneath the rocky ridge that leads up to Ben Tianavaig.

Opposite Holoman Island the road bears right and climbs to a junction. Do not take the first turn to the left, which is a dead end, but continue to the next and cross a cattle-grid before turning left at a T-junction **B**. This road climbs briefly but then drops down to cross a burn. After another short climb it levels out and reaches a large layby **C**, where there is a picnic seat. A good clear path

0	200	400	600	800 METRES	1	
						KILOMETRES
						MILES
0	200	400	600 YARDS	½		

Raasay

leaves from this layby. Dùn Caan suddenly comes into view on the left after about quarter of an hour on this path. Soon after this the path reaches a lochan below the summit **D**.

Walk round the lochan and descend a steep rock staircase on to a path going down to Loch na Meilich. Walk round the southern shore of the loch, where there is a notice-board, and then take the path that zigzags to the summit of Dùn Caan **E** at 1470ft (448m). Boswell made the ascent in 1773 and is supposed to have danced a reel on the summit.

When you have finished enjoying the wonderful view, return on the path to the notice-board at the head of the loch and retrace your steps to the lochan **D**. The route now lies southwards on the top of the ridge, which soon gives views down to the Loch na Mna. There is no obvious path along the ridge. When the latter ends, bear to the right and take the easiest way down, avoiding the steep outcrops of pock-marked rock.

You will have descended from the ridge in a south-westerly direction. It is now necessary to turn south again, so bear left and keep a sharp lookout for cairns built on exposed rock. When you find one of these, look southwards to pick out another – it should lead you to the stream **F** that flows from Loch na Mna and becomes the Inverarish Burn. A well-trodden path runs to the right of the burn. There is a beautiful distant view of the mainland coastline and mountains as you follow the path.

For some way the route is straightforward, but then it becomes more complicated when erosion of the banks of the burn force you to cross to the opposite side. There will probably be several occasions when you cross the stream, but you should be on its southern (left) bank when it reaches the forest.

Now keep the forestry fence to the right as you descend. The view ahead is magical. Keep an eye open for golden eagles, which often hunt on these hills. The path comes to a wooden bridge and then the old mine workings **G**. Cross the road after the ruins, following a footpath waymark that leads to the incline, the track of the railway that carried the iron ore down to the sea. Follow the path down to the piers of the viaduct that took the line over a deep glen. The path descends into the glen, crosses another path and then steeply climbs the opposite slope.

Once at the top, continue to follow the incline but do not, if you wish to return directly to the Ferry Pier, descend to the houses you see below. The incline continues in a straight line to the left of these, and there is a waymark to guide you to the correct path. Cross a fence by an old industrial building (perhaps once an engine house) and continue to follow the incline, here known as the Burma Road because it was built by prisoners of war. This part of the route could hardly be bettered as the path, on springy turf, descends gently with a wonderful panorama of coast and mountain. You can also keep a watchful eye on the ferry as it approaches the slipway just below. ●

Loch na Sealga and Gleann Chaorachain

Start	From the A832 about ½ mile (800m) south of the junction with the Badrallach road
Distance	11 miles (17.5km)
Approximate time	6 hours
Parking	Layby at the orange-painted snow-gate on the A832
Refreshments	None
Ordnance Survey maps	Landranger 19 (Gairloch & Ullapool, Loch Maree) and Pathfinders 120, NH 08/18 (An Teallach & Dundonnell) and 130, NH 07/17 (Loch a' Bhraoin)

This long walk introduces you to one of the grandest mountains of the Northern Highlands, An Teallach, whose pinnacled ridges provide many a challenge for seasoned rock climbers as well as a refuge for golden eagles. However, this route ignores the challenge of its crags and pursues a course round the southern end of the Munro (the principal summit is at 3483ft or 1062m) over a rocky pass to Shenavall, a bothy providing a view of remote Loch na Sealga. If you wish to extend the walk you may like to walk the extra mile (1.5km) to the shore of the lonely loch, using the same path to return to Shenavall. The return is made by following the Abhainn Srath na Sealga upstream to the abandoned cottage of Achneigie. A short way beyond this, a path climbs to the watershed of Sail Liath and then descends Gleann Chaorachain, rejoining the outward route.

The track starts from the southern side of the A832 by the brightly painted snow-gates. The A832 is also known as Destitution Road, having been built in the 1840s to provide relief for local people suffering from the famine that followed the failure of successive potato crops. The track soon reaches a gate by dog-legging up the initial slope and then follows Gleann Chaorachain with the burn to the right and An Teallach's jagged crags beyond. There is a series of waterfalls at tree level – the way can be seen zigzagging up the bare hill ahead, having crossed to the other side of the stream (it is best to cross a little way after the track fords it).

After about 50 minutes of steady ascent, you will reach three cairns (one standing alone, then two more on the right). Take the path leaving to the right here **A** to go between the two cairns. As you climb there are good views of Loch Coire Chaorachain to the left and An

Teallach is suddenly revealed to the right. The going is rough underfoot, soft, moist peaty bits alternating with loose rock.

The view down a valley to the right also comes suddenly but the path heads away from this towards the mountain. At this point it is broad and often vague at times as it swings westwards. A view of Loch na Sealga comes as a surprise when the path comes to a rocky cleft. The path descends steeply to the right of a stream to reach Shenavall **B** – few

bothies can rival its picturesque site, ideally placed to give a human dimension to the prospect of mountain and loch. An unfortunate aspect of human activity here comes from the aircraft which use the glen for low-flying, the planes disappearing into the distance before the sound arrives to deafen you. Deer graze about Shenavall, apparently unaware of the noise of aircraft or the presence of walkers.

If you do not intend to visit the shore of Loch na Sealga, turn left from the bothy, cross the stream and then climb the path which runs above the north bank of the river. The

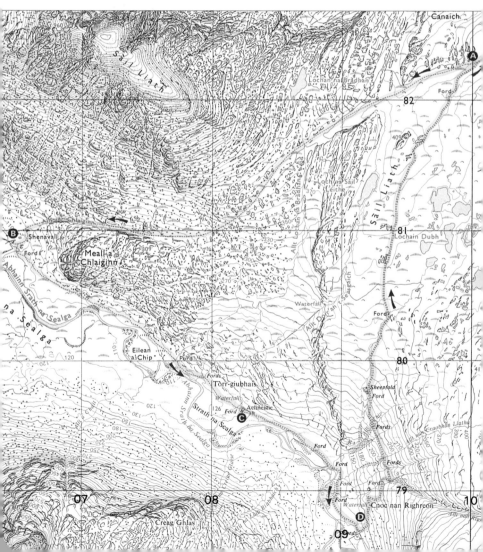

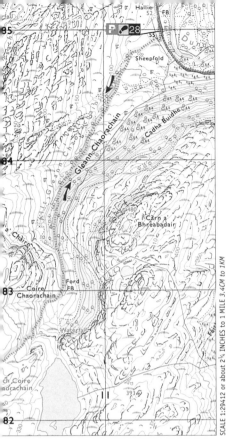

SCALE 1:29412 or about 2¼ INCHES to 1 MILE 3.4CM to 1KM

may depend on the season) and then seems to end abruptly. Go round the gorse patch that faces you at this point and then bear left away from the river to walk across the meadow diagonally to find a track **D** steeply climbing the hill. An incredible view opens up as you climb, passing the site of an abandoned croft. Its former occupants would have enjoyed the view down the valley extending to Loch na Sealga.

After an initial steep climb the walking is enjoyable on a good track, which gives more fine views to the left. Turn occasionally to enjoy the scenery behind you. An Teallach soon comes into sight ahead. Note the remains of ancient tree roots by the track, which show that the landscape here has not always been as barren as its appears today. When you come to a group of lochans to the right, you know that the cairns where the ways parted earlier **A** are not too far distant ahead.

Quite soon after this, at the head of Gleann Chaorachain, the track descends more steeply to run for a short way by the side of the refreshing burn. Once you come to the trees it is only about a mile (1.5km) before you reach the starting point and the main road. ●

building on the opposite side of the glen is Larachantivore, a cottage which is reserved for fishing and stalking parties. The mountain behind is Beinn Dearg Mór (2974ft/908m), with its two curving ridges meeting below a conical summit. Cattle graze the meadows by the river, and it is interesting to think of them being driven out before the winter, or alternatively are they sent down the loch by boat? Lower, less spectacular hills face you as you approach Achneigie **C**, its seven chimneys coming into view in a somewhat puzzling way before the rest of the house is seen. There is a beautiful waterfall close to the farmhouse, the latter sadly becoming ruinous.

Take the Land Rover track from Achneigie, which follows the course of the river. The track crosses two fords (four according to the map, it

Achneigie and Beinn Dearg Mór

Further Information

The Law and Tradition as they affect Walking in Scotland

Walkers following the routes given in this book should not run into problems, but it is as well to know something about the law as it affects access, and also something of the traditions which can be quite different in Scotland from elsewhere in Britain. Most of this is common sense, observing the country code and having consideration for other people and their activities which, after all, may be their livelihood.

It is often said that there is no law of trespass in Scotland. In fact there is, but the trespass itself is not usually a criminal offence. You can be asked to leave any property, and technically 'reasonable force' may be used to obtain your compliance – though the term is not defined! You can be charged with causing damage due to the trespass, but this would be hard to establish if you were just walking on

The unblemished beach at Sandwood Bay

open, wild, hilly country where, whatever the law, in practice there has been a long tradition of free access for recreational walking – something both the Scottish Landowners' Federation and the Mountaineering Council of Scotland do not want to see changed.

There are certain restrictions. Walkers should obey the country code and seasonal restrictions arising from lambing or stalking. Where there is any likelihood of such restrictions this is mentioned in the text and visitors are asked to comply. When camping, use a campsite. Camp fires should not be lit; they are a danger to moorland and forest, and really not necessary as lightweight and efficient stoves are now available.

Many of the walks in this book are on rights of way. The watchdog on rights of way in Scotland is the Scottish Rights of Way Society (SRWS), who maintain details on all established cases and will, if need be, contest attempted closures. They produce a booklet on the Scottish legal position (Rights of Way, A Guide to the Law in Scotland, 1991),

and their green signposts are a familiar sight by many footpaths and tracks, indicating the lines of historic routes.

In Scotland rights of way are not marked on Ordnance Survey maps as is the case south of the border. It was not felt necessary to show these as such on the maps – a further reflection of the freedom to roam that is enjoyed in Scotland. So a path on a map is no indication of a right of way, and many paths and tracks of great use to walkers were built by estates as stalking paths or for private access. While you may traverse such paths, taking due care to avoid damage to property and the natural environment, you should obey restricted access notices and leave if asked to do so.

The only established rights of way are those where a court case has resulted in a legal judgment, but there are thousands of other 'claimed' rights of way. Local planning authorities have a duty to protect rights of way – no easy task with limited resources. Many attempts at closing claimed rights of way have been successfully contested in the courts by the Scottish Rights of Way Society and local authorities.

A dog on a lead or under control may also be taken on a right of way. There is little chance of meeting a free-range solitary bull on any of the walks. Any herds seen are not likely to be dairy cattle, but all cows can be inquisitive and may approach walkers, especially if they have a dog. Dogs running among stock may be shot on the spot; this is not draconian legislation but a desperate attempt to stop sheep and lambs being harmed, driven to panic or lost, sometimes with fatal results. Any practical points or restrictions

applicable will be made in the text of each walk. If there is no comment it can be assumed that the route carries no real restrictions.

Scotland in fact likes to keep everything as natural as possible, so, for

Beinn na Callich, Skye

instance. waymarking is kept to a minimum (the Scottish Rights of Way Society signposts and Forest Walk markers are in unobtrusive colours). In Scotland people are asked to 'walk softly in the wilderness, to take nothing except photographs, and leave nothing except footprints' – which is better than any law.

Scotland's Hills and Mountains: a Concordat on Access

This remarkable agreement was published early in 1996 and is likely to have considerable influence on walkers' rights in Scotland in the future. The signatories include organisations which have formerly been at odds - the Scottish Landowners' Federation and the Ramblers' Association, for example. However they joined with others to make the Access Forum (a full list of signatories is detailed below). The RSPB and the National Trust for Scotland did not sign the Concordat initially but it is hoped that they will support its principles.

The signatories of the Concordat are:

Association of Deer Management
　Groups
Convention of Scottish Local
　Authorities
Mountaineering Council of Scotland
National Farmers' Union of Scotland
Ramblers' Association Scotland
Scottish Countryside Activities Council
Scottish Landowners' Federation
Scottish Natural Heritage
Scottish Sports Association
Scottish Sports Council

They agreed that the basis of access to the hills for the purposes of informal recreation should be:

Freedom of access exercised with responsibility and subject to reasonable constraints for management and conservation purposes.

Looking back to Shenaval

Acceptance by visitors of the needs of land management, and understanding of how this sustains the livelihood, culture and community interests of those who live and work in the hills.

Acceptance by land managers of the public's expectation of having access to the hills.

Acknowledgment of a common interest in the natural beauty and special qualities of Scotland's hills, and the need to work together for their protection and enhancement.

The Forum point out that the success of the Concordat will depend on all who manage or visit the hills acting on these four principles. In addition, the parties to the Concordat will promote good practice in the form of:

Courtesy and consideration at a personal level.

A welcome to visitors.

Making advice readily available on the ground or in advance.

Better information about the uplands and hill land uses through environmental education.

Respect by visitors for the welfare needs of livestock and wildlife.

Adherence to relevant codes and standards of good practice by visitors and land managers alike.

Any local restrictions on access should be essential for the needs of management, should be fully explained, and be for the minimum period and area required.

Queries should be addressed to:
Access Forum Secretariat,
c/o Recreation and Access Branch,
Scottish Natural Heritage,
2 Anderson Place, Edinburgh EH6 5NP.

 Safety on the Hills

The Highland hills and lower but remote areas call for care and respect. The idyllic landscape of the tourist brochures can change rapidly into a world of gales, rain and mist, potentially lethal for those ill-equipped or lacking navigational skills. The Scottish hills in winter can be arctic in severity, and even in summer, snow can lash the summits.

At the very least carry adequate wind- and waterproof outer garments, food and drink to spare, a basic first-aid kit, whistle, map and compass – and know how to use them. Wear boots. Plan within your capabilities. If going alone ensure you leave details of your proposed route. Heed local advice, listen to weather forecasts, and do not hesitate to modify plans if conditions deteriorate.

Some of the walks in this book venture into remote country and others climb high summits, and these expeditions should only be undertaken in good summer conditions. In winter they could well need the skills and experience of mountaineering rather than walking. In midwinter the hours of daylight are of course much curtailed, but given crisp, clear late-winter days many of the shorter expeditions would be perfectly feasible, if the guidelines given are adhered to.

Mountain Rescue
In case of emergency the standard procedure is to dial 999 and ask for the police who will assess and deal with the situation.

First, however, render first aid as required and make sure the casualty is made warm and comfortable. The distress signal (six flashes/whistle-blasts, repeated at minute intervals) may bring help from other walkers in the area. Write down essential details: exact location (six-figure reference), time of accident, numbers involved, details of injuries, steps already taken; then despatch a messenger to phone the police.

If leaving the casualty alone, mark the site with an eye-catching object. Be patient; waiting for help can seem interminable.

 Useful Organisations

Association for the Protection of Rural Scotland
Gladstone's Land, 3rd floor,
483 Lawnmarket, Edinburgh EH1 2NT.
Tel. 0131 225 7012
Forestry Commission
Information Dept, 231 Corstorphine Rd,
Edinburgh EH12 7AT. Tel. 0131 334 0303
Historic Scotland
Longmore House, Salibury Place,
Edinburgh EH9 1SH. Tel. 0131 668 8600
Long Distance Walkers' Association
21 Upcroft, Windsor, Berkshire SL4 3NH.
Tel. 01753 866685
National Trust for Scotland
5 Charlotte Square, Edinburgh
EH2 4DU. Tel. 0131 226 5922
Ordnance Survey
Romsey Road, Southampton SO16 4GU.
Tel. 08456 05 05 05 (Lo-call)
Ramblers' Association (Scotland)
23 Crusader House, Haig Business Park,
Markinch, Fife KY7 6AQ.
Tel. 01592 611177

Royal Society for the
Protection of Birds
Abernethy Forest Reserve, Forest Lodge,
Nethybridge, Inverness-shire PH25 3EF.
Tel. 01479 821409
Scottish Natural Heritage
Information and Library Services,
2 Anderson Place,
Edinburgh EH6 5NP.
Tel. 0131 554 9797

Scottish Rights of Way Society Ltd
John Cotton Business Centre,
10/2 Sunnyside, Edinburgh EH7 5RA.
Tel. 0131 652 2937
Scottish Wildlife Trust
Cramond House, Cramond Glebe Road,
Edinburgh EH4 6NS. Tel. 0131 312 7765
Scottish Youth Hostels Association
7 Glebe Crescent, Stirling FK8 2JA.
Tel. 01786 451181

 ## Glossary of Gaelic Names

Most of the place-names in this region are Gaelic in origin, and this list gives
some of the more common elements, which will allow readers to understand
otherwise meaningless words and appreciate the relationship between place-
names and landscape features. Place-names often have variant spellings, and the
more common of these are given here.

aber	mouth of loch, river	eilidh	hind
abhainn	river	eòin, eun	bird
allt	stream	fionn	white
auch, ach	field	fraoch	heather
bal, bail, baile	town, homestead	gabhar, ghabhar,	
bàn	white, fair, pale	gobhar	goat
bealach	hill pass	garbh	rough
beg, beag	small	geal	white
ben, beinn	hill	ghlas, glas	grey
bhuidhe	yellow	gleann, glen	narrow, valley
blar	plain	gorm	blue, green
brae, braigh	upper slope,	inbhir, inver	confluence
	steepening	inch, inis, innis	island, meadow by
breac	speckled		river
cairn	pile of stones, often	lag, laggan	hollow
	marking a summit	làrach	old site
cam	crooked	làirig	pass
càrn	cairn, cairn-shaped	leac	slab
	hill	liath	grey
caol, kyle	strait	loch	lake
ceann, ken, kin	head	lochan	small loch
cil, kil	church, cell	màm	pass, rise
clach	stone	maol	bald-shaped top
clachan	small village	monadh	upland, moor
cnoc	hill, knoll, knock	mór, mor(e)	big
coille, killie	wood	odhar, odhair	dun-coloured
corrie, coire,		rhu, rubha	point
choire	mountain hollow	ruadh	red, brown
craig, creag	cliff, crag	sgòr, sgòrr,	
crannog,		sgùrr	pointed
crannag	man-made island	sron	nose
dàl, dail	field, flat	stob	pointed
damh	stag	strath	valley (broader than
dearg	red		glen)
druim, drum	long ridge	tarsuinn	traverse, across
dubh, dhu	black, dark	tom	hillock (rounded)
dùn	hill fort	tòrr	hillock (more rugged)
eas	waterfall	tulloch, tulach	knoll
eilean	island	uisge	water, river

**Tourist Information
Centres**
Highlands of Scotland
Tourist Board:
Tel. 01997 421160
*Local tourist information
numbers*:
Broadford, Isle of Skye:
01471 822361
Durness: 01971 511259
Gairloch: 01445 712130
Kyle of Lochalsh:
01599 534276
Lochcarron: 01520
722357
Lochinver: 01571 844330
Mallaig: 01687 462170
Portree, Isle of Skye:
01478 612137
Uig, Isle of Skye:
01470 542404
Ullapool: 01854 612135

Stac Pollaidh at dusk, Loch Col Dromannan

Weather Forecasts
Mountaincall West
Tel. 0891 500441
Scotland seven-day forecast
Tel. 0891 112260
UK seven-day forecast
Tel. 0891 333123

 *Ordnance Survey Maps
of Skye and the North West
Highlands*
The walks described in this guide are
covered by Ordnance Survey 1:50,000
scale (1 $\frac{1}{4}$ inches to 1 mile or 2cm to
1km) Landranger map sheets 9, 15, 19,
23, 24, 32.

These all-purpose maps are packed
with information to help you explore
the area. Viewpoints, picnic sites, places
of interest and caravan and camping
sites are shown, as well as public rights
of way information such as footpaths
and bridleways.

To examine the area in more detail,
especially if you are planning walks,
the Ordnance Survey Outdoor Leisure
maps at 1:25 000 scale (2 $\frac{1}{2}$ inches to
1 mile or 4cm to 1km) are ideal. Maps

covering the area are: Sheet 8 The
Cuillin and Torridon Hills.

Pathfinder maps also at 1:25,000 scale
cover the area:

43 (NC16/26)	130 (NH07/17)
52 (NC15)	138 (NG46/56)
72 (NC03/13)	152 (NG14/15)
83 (NC22/32)	154 (NG45/55)
109 (NG78/79)	155 (NG65/75)
110 (NG89/99)	171 (NG44/54)
119 (NG88/98)	187 (NG43/53)
120 (NH08/18)	202 (NG32)
127 (NG37/47)	234 (NG50)
129 (NG87/97)	235 (NG60/70)

To get to Skye and the North West
Highlands use the Ordnance Survey
Great Britain Routeplanner (Travel-
master map number 1) or Travelmaster
map 2 Northern Scotland, Travelmaster
map 3 Western Scotland and Western
Isles, Travelmaster map 4 Central
Scotland and Northumberland.

Ordnance Survey maps and guides
are available from most booksellers,
stationers and newsagents.

Index

Entries in italic type refer to illustrations